COPYRIGHT

©Tektra 2002
No part of this workbook may be copied, photocopied or reproduced in any form or by
any means without written permission from Tektra Ltd.

Such permission can be obtained from:

Tektra Ltd
Unit 4A, Gateway Business Park
Beancross Road
Grangemouth
FK3 8WX

LIMITATION OF LIABILITY

All reasonable precautions have been taken to ensure complete and accurate
information concerning the material presented in this workbook. However, Tektra Ltd
cannot be held legally responsible for any errors or omissions in printing or faulty
instructions contained within this workbook. If you find any errors in this workbook,
please inform Tektra Ltd. Whilst every effort is made to eradicate typing or technical
mistakes, we apologise for any errors you may detect. Your feedback is both valued by
us and will help us to maintain the highest possible standards.

Information within this workbook is subject to change without notice. Companies,
names and data used in examples herein are fictitious unless otherwise noted.

There are no warranties, expressed or implied, including warranties of merchantability
or fitness for a particular purpose, made with respect to the materials or any information
provided to the user herein. Neither the author nor publisher shall be liable for any
direct, indirect, special, incidental or consequential damages arising out of the use or
inability to use the content of this workbook.

Screen shots reprinted by permission from Microsoft Corporation.

Introduction to Presentation Graphics

Before working through this *Presentation Graphics* resource pack it is important that you read the following information that has been written to offer you guidance on how to get the best out of this resource pack.

The resource pack has been divided into units. Each unit consists of a number of IT-related categories. Throughout these categories are tasks, designed to help you understand how to use the computer and how the different parts of a computer work.

At your own pace, you are required to read through the resource pack, learning about different aspects of the computer and how it is used to help understand the important and basic principles of Information Technology.

At key moments throughout the resource pack you will be instructed to perform a practical assignment or task. These tasks are there to demonstrate, with a practical hands-on approach, the important theoretical aspects of the computer that might otherwise be difficult to understand merely by reading through the resource pack.

It is important that you carefully read through each category before attempting to do the tasks, as this will equip you with the knowledge you will need to answer the questions contained within each task.

Don't worry if occasionally you find yourself having to refer back to the section you have just read in order to complete a task. Only through reading each category and completing the accompanying tasks will you correctly learn about the principles of Presentation Graphics.

Consolidation exercises are also contained within each resource pack. These exercises provide a further opportunity to re-cap the various categories and tasks that you will have previously undertaken, while earlier working through the resource pack.

By following these simple instructions and correctly using this resource pack, you will find that learning about the principles of Presentation Graphics will be far more enjoyable and so much easier.

Contents

On completion of this unit you will have learnt about:

- **An Introduction To Presentation Graphics Using Microsoft PowerPoint 2000**

  - PowerPoint Output Options
  - On Screen Presentations
  - Web Pages For Web Use
  - Colour And Black And White Overheads And Paper Printouts
  - 35mm Slides
  - Audience Handouts
  - Speaker Notes

- **System Requirements**

  - Hardware
  - Software

- **The Keyboard In Detail**

©Tektra TEKPG1RP1102

An Introduction To Presentation Graphics Using Microsoft PowerPoint 2000

PowerPoint 2000 can be used to develop your presentation ideas visually on the computer and to capture the attention of your audience. With this type of software you can create handouts, overheads (to be used with an overhead projector) and charts.

A presentation is a series of related slides that together can make up an electronic slideshow (a list of slides displayed sequentially on screen or using a projection device such as an overhead projector, like a photographic slide show).

Presentations may be used in the following situations:

*   Informal or formal meetings
*   Presenting information to an audience
*   Delivering your ideas or messages over the Internet
*   Advertising/selling a product
*   Presenting a business plan or proposed idea
*   Training/teaching

To make the presentation as effective as possible, visual effects can be used to bring your data to life! There are many tools within the application that enable you to do this, such as:

*   Inserting text in different styles, colours and sizes
*   Inserting Clip Art & photographs
*   Inserting sounds
*   Inserting movie clips
*   Inserting charts

Making the most of the resources around us can help in the creation of a presentation. Graphics, sounds, photographs and movie clips can be found on the Internet, making it a powerful resource.

With the increase in the use of digital cameras, scanners and camcorders, these resources can also be incorporated into the presentation.

To learn more about presentation graphics this resource pack uses an application called **Microsoft PowerPoint 2000** which is a component of **Microsoft Office 2000**.

This module allows you to put your ideas onto the screen and transform them into something which will have a visual impact on your audience.

PowerPoint Output Options

A presentation consists of a series of slides that when put together make up an electronic slide show or presentation. Each slide is like a page in a document and can be edited. An example of a series of slides in a presentation is shown below:

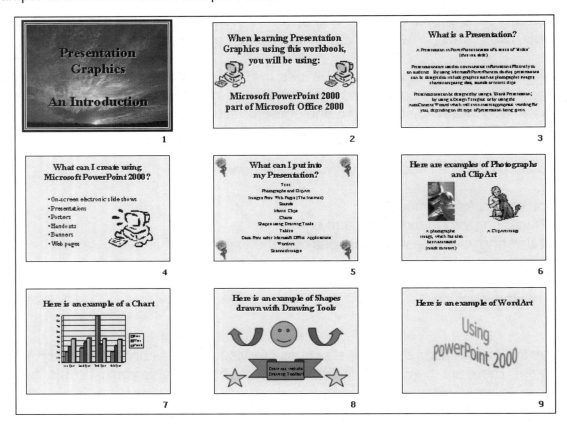

You have already learned of some of the most common situations where PowerPoint presentations are used, but what format should you choose when presenting? This section will take a closer look at the options available to you, using PowerPoint 2000.

On Screen Presentations

You can create and edit a complete presentation and use Slide View to rehearse the slide show before actually showing it electronically to an audience. This will allow you to completely check the whole presentation and to rehearse the actual timings of each slide. If you use this method you can take advantage of the advanced features available within PowerPoint such as animation (movement), transition (effects added between slide changeovers), sound and movies.

You will need a suitably sized monitor or screen on which to electronically present the slide show, or you can use a special overhead projector that will allow a computer and projector to be connected together. The screen image is then projected into a large image on a white screen.

Web Pages For Web Use

You don't need to be a web page author to publish your presentation on the Internet for the world to view. You can select the option to **Save as Web Page** from the **File** menu and your presentation will be converted into the language that the Internet recognises (HTML – Hypertext Mark-up Language). Your presentation should not look very different, though some formatting may have been adjusted to suit the new layout.

Once saved in this format you are free to upload it onto a current web page or use the presentation as the web page. Your friends and/or colleagues can view your presentation over the Internet using a web browser.

Colour And Black And White Overheads And Paper Printouts

Slides can be created in colour within PowerPoint, but at any point during the creating and editing of the presentation you can view what the presentation will look like in greyscale or black and white. Slides can be printed onto overhead transparency paper that is a clear plastic-like material used with overhead projectors.

Overhead projectors are so named because they 'project' something over the level of people's heads, so that the whole audience can view what is being presented. They consist of a large box with a clear top for placing the transparencies onto and a stem containing a powerful and expensive bulb. When switched on, the light 'projects' through the paper laying on the top and puts the image on the nearest surface, for example a wall. For this reason a screen is used (usually white) that is on wheels and can be used anywhere.

Before printing any transparencies using the slides in your presentation you must check that your printer is capable of printing to this type of special paper. If it is not, you will end up with a very sticky and ruined roller in your printer!

This method of printing a presentation is common in schools and colleges, where this equipment is in common use.

Alternatively you can print the slides directly onto plain paper in colour, greyscale or pure black and white. You may wish to talk your audience through the presentation rather than projecting it anywhere.

35mm Slides

There are specialised businesses that can transfer your presentation onto 35mm slides. You will need to research this in your local area. There is also specialised equipment that is used to display the slides and project them for an audience to view.

Audience Handouts

Handouts are particularly useful to give out to members of the audience during and/or at the end of a presentation. They consist of miniatures of the slides contained in the presentation on a piece of paper. You can choose how many slides per page to display or to add note space for the audience to add their own notes.

Speaker Notes

If you are the speaker or the presenter of a presentation you can add electronic notes for particular slides or all slides. You can print the slides using the Notes Page layout and have them to hand whilst presenting to an audience. Alternatively you can view the notes whilst showing the presentation, using settings that allow only you to view the notes and not your audience.

TASK

On a separate sheet of paper, answer the following questions:

1. Name three situations where an electronic presentation can be used.

2. Name four presentation effects that can be used to enhance an electronic presentation.

3. What advantages are there when saving your presentation as a web page?

4. In your opinion, exploring the PowerPoint output options, which method would be the most effective in presenting to an audience?

System Requirements

To use Microsoft PowerPoint 2000 you will need the hardware and software described below. This will enable you to fully use the features within it. Consider the following recommendations before using Microsoft PowerPoint 2000.

Hardware

You will need a **personal** or **multimedia computer** with input devices such as the **keyboard** and **mouse** (pointing device). Your **monitor** (screen) should be at least VGA or higher-resolution video adapter (Super VGA 256-colour recommended). The computer should contain a 486 processor or higher.

A **printer** (output device), either colour or black and white (monochrome). Slides are produced mainly in colour on the screen so a colour printer may be more beneficial, but this will depend on the quality of the colour printer.

A **CD-ROM** drive. This will enable you to access large libraries of Clip Art for incorporation into your presentation.

The **memory** in your computer should be at least 8 megabytes (Mb) of RAM (Random Access Memory) for use on Windows 95 and 16 Mb for use on a Windows NT Workstation. Most recent systems will contain much more than this minimum requirement.

You will require 26–58 Mb of available **hard-disk space**; 43 Mb is required for a typical installation, depending on configuration (use the Office Upgrade Wizard during setup to maximize free disk space).

Optional hardware items include the following:

A **modem** for gaining access to the Internet for additional resources. A minimum modem speed of 14.4k is recommended.

A multimedia computer will have the added benefit of incorporating **speakers** and a **microphone** for use with sounds in presentations. Microphones can be particularly useful for recording the speaker's voice.

Software

The **operating system** on your computer should be at least Microsoft Windows® 95 or Microsoft Windows NT® Workstation 3.51 (incorporating Service Pack 5 or later). The software will not run on earlier versions of this software.

Internet access is an optional requirement as this can provide access to extra features contained within PowerPoint. However, be aware that a separate access fee may be charged.

The Keyboard In Detail

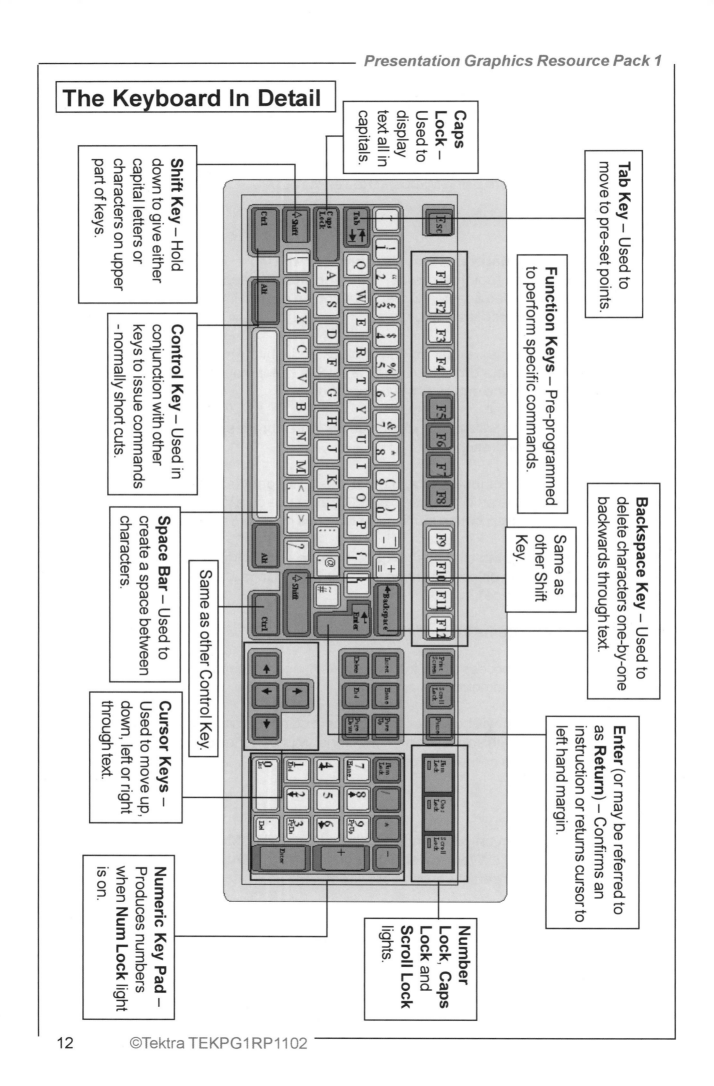

Caps Lock – Used to display text all in capitals.

Shift Key – Hold down to give either capital letters or characters on upper part of keys.

Control Key – Used in conjunction with other keys to issue commands - normally short cuts.

Space Bar – Used to create a space between characters.

Same as other Control Key.

Cursor Keys – Used to move up, down, left or right through text.

Numeric Key Pad – Produces numbers when **Num Lock** light is on.

Tab Key – Used to move to pre-set points.

Function Keys – Pre-programmed to perform specific commands.

Backspace Key – Used to delete characters one-by-one backwards through text.

Same as other Shift Key.

Enter (or may be referred to as **Return**) – Confirms an instruction or returns cursor to left hand margin.

Number Lock, Caps Lock and **Scroll Lock** lights.

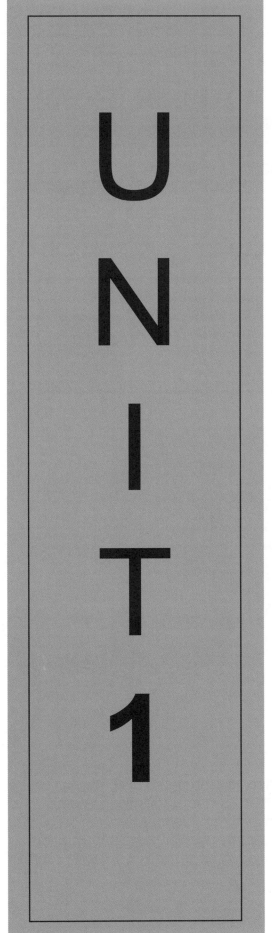

On completion of this unit you will have learnt about and practised:

- **Opening PowerPoint 2000**

- **Opening An Existing Presentation**

  - Templates
  - The Advantages Of Using Design Templates
  - Blank Presentation

- **Help**

- **Saving Presentations**

- **Closing Presentations**

- **Closing PowerPoint 2000**

Opening PowerPoint 2000

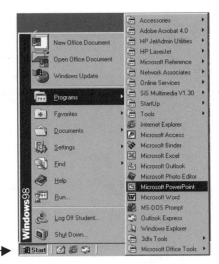

Click on the **Start** button on the Windows taskbar.
Click **Programs**.
Click **Microsoft PowerPoint**.

Locate the **Start** button at
the bottom left of the
Desktop

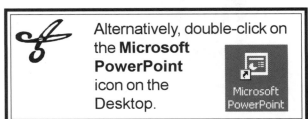

Alternatively, double-click on
the **Microsoft**
PowerPoint
icon on the
Desktop.

The following screen will appear (Fig 1):

The options available when opening
Microsoft PowerPoint 2000 are:

- **AutoContent Wizard**
- **Design Template**
- **Blank presentation**
- **Open an existing presentation**

Fig 1

AutoContent Wizard

A Wizard is a series of step by step screens guiding you through a task. If you require
sample content to help you with your presentation, then use the AutoContent Wizard. This
is a quick and easy way to create presentations in minutes. Using a minimal amount of
information such as the type of presentation, how it will be used and the output options, a
presentation can be created. By pressing **Next** at each step, the Wizard will progress
through a series of questions.

Templates

When you select the **Design Template** option, a choice of pre-defined styles can be selected. To choose a style, click once with the left mouse button on any of the icons. The preview will appear on the right. Click **OK** once you have chosen your style.

The Advantages Of Using Design Templates

One of the major tasks in creating a new presentation is making it look consistent and professional. PowerPoint recognises this and so provides an extensive range of design templates that can be used to construct a presentation in this way.

There are many different templates to select from, including business type presentation layouts. You can apply a design template at any time during the creation of a presentation using the **Format**, **Apply Design Template** option from the menu bar. This allows you to experiment with different designs using your content.

Design templates use the same colour scheme, font size and type throughout a presentation. This makes it look professional. The advantage of using this type of method is that you can also customise the presentation to include your own styles as well as those from the template.

Blank Presentation

A blank presentation will allow you to design your own presentation.

The **New Slide** dialogue box will appear:

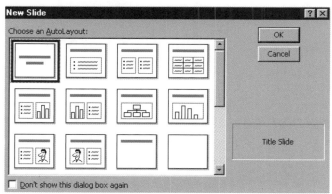

Choose an AutoLayout for the first slide in your presentation. Notice the different layouts available. Selections can be made by clicking on the **AutoLayout** with the left mouse button. A thick border will appear around the selected layout.

Click **OK** once a layout has been selected and the layout will be displayed on slide 1 of your presentation.

Opening An Existing Presentation

When selecting the **Open an existing presentation** option, the **Open** dialogue box will appear (Fig 2).

PowerPoint needs to know the location in which to find your presentation.

Click on the drop-down arrow to the right of the **Look in:** box and select **3½ Floppy (A:)**

Ensure that you have a disk in the computer.

To select a presentation, point to it and click the left mouse button. Click on the **Open** button.

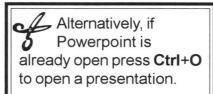

Alternatively, if Powerpoint is already open press **Ctrl+O** to open a presentation.

Fig 2

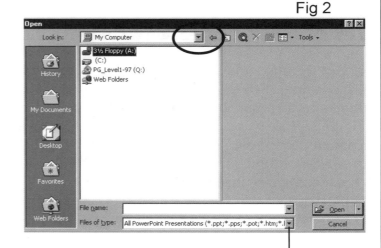

Ensure that **Files of type** reads **All PowerPoint Presentations**
If this is not showing, click on the drop-down arrow and select All PowerPoint Presentations.

T A S K

1.   *Start PowerPoint.*

2.   *Open the existing presentation called **Introductory Presentation 2000**.*

Help

The Microsoft suite has an excellent system to help you when you perhaps can't remember how to do something, or are not sure what something on the screen is for. There are two types of help:

- Context-sensitive help
- Office Assistant

Context-sensitive help

This enables you to point at any part of the screen, including toolbars and menu bars, and you will be given information about its name and what it is used for. To do this you need first of all to press **Shift+F1**. Your mouse pointer will then change to an arrow and question mark. Point at any part of the screen that you wish to find out about and click the left-hand mouse button.

Office Assistant

The Office Assistant provides help and gives tips to enable you to accomplish your tasks.

To start Office Assistant click the **Office Assistant** button on the toolbar.
If the **Office Assistant** does not appear, go to **Help/Show The Office Assistant**.

Click on the **Office Assistant**.

The Office Assistant ————————

Type your question in here and then click on the **Search** option.

The Office Assistant will then give you options to select, depending on your question. Select an option and the help will be displayed.

T **A** **S** **K**	1. *Activate the Office Assistant in PowerPoint.* 2. *Search for help on **PowerPoint Views**.* 3. *What are the five different types of view?* 4. *Search for help on **Starting A Slide Show from within PowerPoint**.* 5. *What help do you get? Are there clear instructions on how to carry this out? If so, how is it done?* 6. *Search for help on **Adding Text to a Placeholder**.* 7. *What information is displayed?*

Saving Presentations

When saving a presentation, you are keeping it permanently and are able to retrieve it at any time. The application allows you to name a presentation so as to identify and organise your documents clearly.

Click **File** from the menu bar; there are three save options:

- **Save**
- **Save As**
- **Save as Web Page**

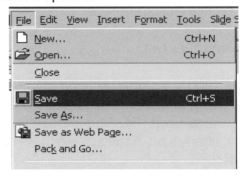

Save

To update a document, use **Save**. This will overwrite the existing copy and the document will keep the same name.

> Alternatively, press **Ctrl+S** to display the Save As dialogue box.

If you selected a blank presentation and have created your presentation from scratch, when you select **File** and **Save**, you will get the **Save As** dialogue box. This is described below and is used to name the presentation.

Save As

When opening an existing presentation and making alterations, you may want to keep both versions. Use **Save As** in this situation. The original copy will save with the original name and the second version will be saved with the new name. The second version can be stored in a different location to the first.

The **Save As** dialogue box (Fig 3).

Ensure that the location to **Save in:** reads **3½ Floppy (A:)** This can be selected by clicking on the drop-down arrow.

The **File name** will state the existing file name. To change this, click in the box with the left mouse button and type a new one.

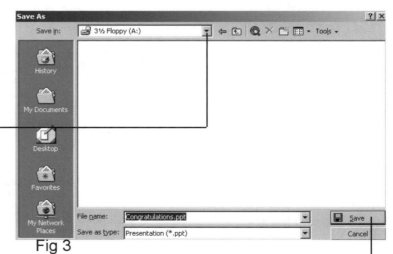

Fig 3

When all save information has been entered, click on the **Save** button.

Save as a Web Page

HTML is an abbreviation of 'Hypertext Mark-up Language', one of the languages used to create web pages for the Internet. By selecting this option, PowerPoint will save your presentation document as a web page.

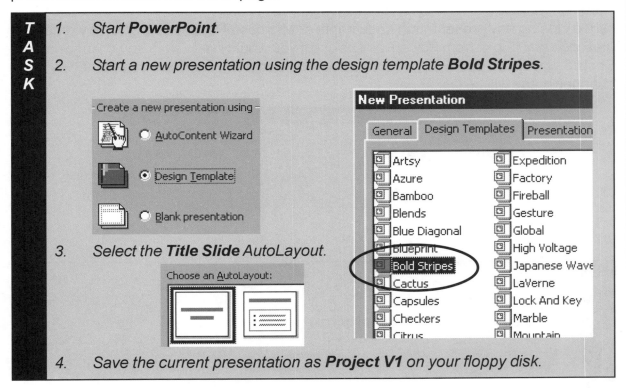

TASK

1.   Start **PowerPoint**.

2.   Start a new presentation using the design template **Bold Stripes**.

3.   Select the **Title Slide** AutoLayout.

4.   Save the current presentation as **Project V1** on your floppy disk.

Closing Presentations

To close a presentation document, click **File** and **Close** from the menu bar.

This method will close your presentation document without closing the Microsoft PowerPoint application, which will remain open on the screen, with no active presentation document.

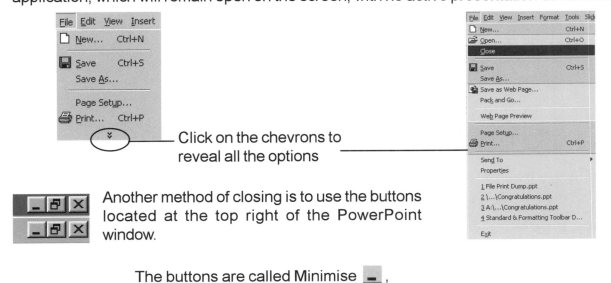

Click on the chevrons to reveal all the options

Another method of closing is to use the buttons located at the top right of the PowerPoint window.

The buttons are called Minimise ▬ , Restore 🗗 and Close ✖

The bottom row of buttons controls the active presentation document on screen.

Closing Microsoft PowerPoint 2000

To close Microsoft PowerPoint, either select **File**, **Exit** from the menu bar or click on the **Close** button at the top right of the PowerPoint window.

When closing any presentation documents or Microsoft PowerPoint, you may receive a message box (Fig 4) from PowerPoint asking if you would like to save any changes made. Ensure you click **Yes** if you have made amendments to your document, otherwise any changes made will be lost.

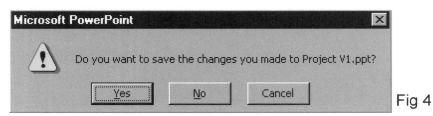

Fig 4

T A S K	1.	*Close all open presentations.*
	2.	*Close Microsoft PowerPoint.*

 ©Tektra TEKPG1RP1102

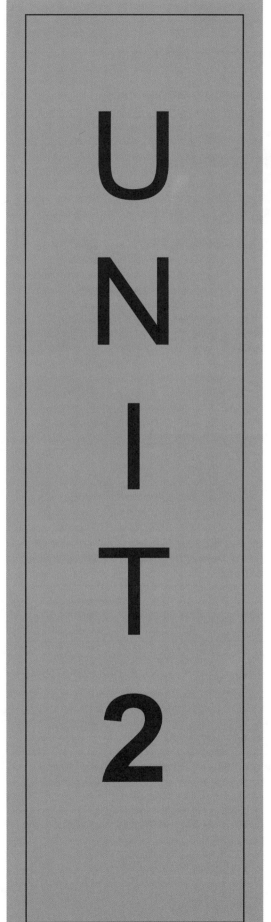

On completion of this unit you will have learnt about and practised the following:

- **The PowerPoint Window**

- **PowerPoint Toolbars**

  - The Standard Toolbar
  - The Formatting Toolbar

- **Navigating PowerPoint 2000**

  - Page Magnification And Zoom
  - Changing Slide Views
  - Moving Around The PowerPoint Screen

The PowerPoint Window

Before you create your own presentation document using PowerPoint, it is important to understand the layout of the PowerPoint window. PowerPoint contains many features and tools which will assist you when creating a presentation.

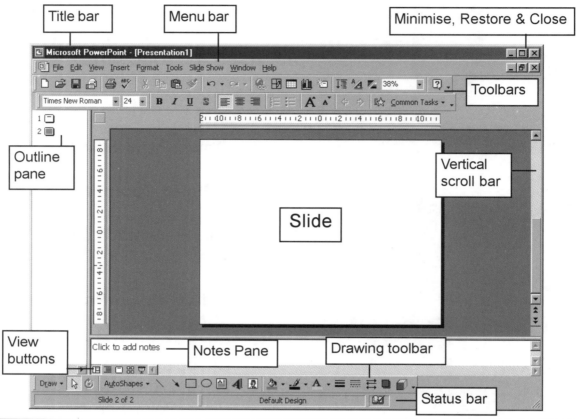

Title bar	The title bar displays the name of the active application together with the filename of the active document. If you have a document open but have not saved, the application will assign a temporary filename such as P**resentation1**.
Minimise, Restore & Close	**Minimise** will 'hide' the active application or document from view. **Restore** will restore a window to its previous size and location. **Close** will close an active document or application.
Menu bar	The menu bar is a special toolbar which displays a menu of 'controls' which, when selected, display a 'drop-down box' of commands. The menu bar can be customised to display other commands regularly used.
Toolbars	There are various types of toolbar available for use with PowerPoint. They consist of a series of buttons and menus, each representing a command. You can add buttons which you use regularly or remove ones which you seldom use.
Vertical scroll bar	The vertical scroll bar will allow you to navigate up and down the active slide. If your presentation document contains multiple slides, then movement between slides can be achieved by using the vertical scroll bar.
Horizontal scroll bar	The horizontal scroll bar will allow you to navigate left and right through your slide if you have a high zoom setting.
Status bar	The first section of the status bar will indicate the active slide you are working on ie Slide 1 of 1. The next section will give information on the name of the design used. If a design template has not been used, it will display 'default design'. The small box to the right of this, if 'double-clicked' with the mouse, will spell check your presentation document.

The PowerPoint Toolbars

There should always be two toolbars displayed in PowerPoint, the **Standard** toolbar and the **Formatting** toolbar. To check which toolbars are displayed, select **View** from the menu bar, and click **Toolbars**. Ensure that **Standard** and **Formatting** are ticked.

Point the mouse at a button on the toolbar (without clicking). A **Tooltip** will be displayed. This is a label letting you know the name or function of a button.

The Standard Toolbar

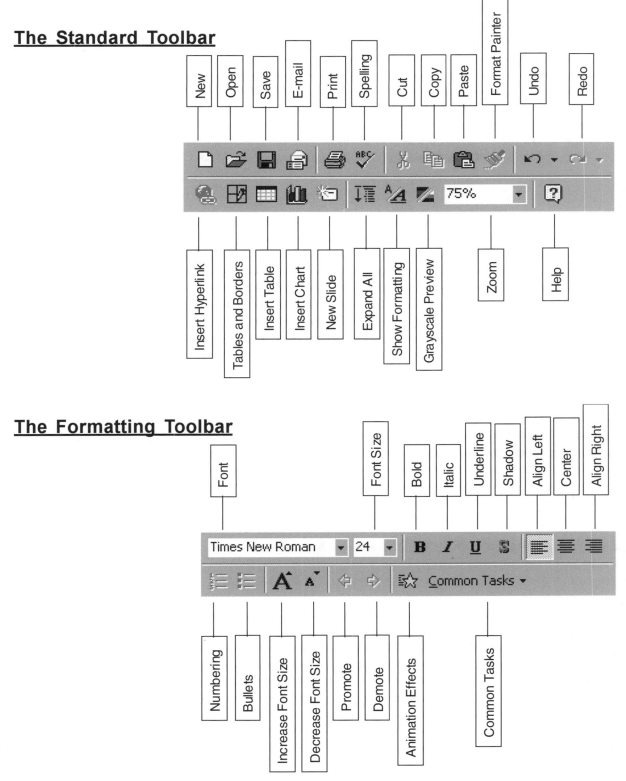

The Formatting Toolbar

Navigating PowerPoint 2000

Page Magnification And Zoom

PowerPoint has a magnification and zoom facility built in and it works together with the scroll bars. It is possible to 'zoom' in and out just like a camera would, to bring an object closer or further away. When working on an object in detail on a slide, you may find it useful to zoom in and make the object larger and easier to work with.

Use either of the following methods to alter the zoom setting for a presentation.

Click **View** from the menu bar, click **Zoom**; the **Zoom** dialogue box will appear:

Notice the different percentage levels available.

This dialogue box indicates that the slide is currently on 76% of the actual size.

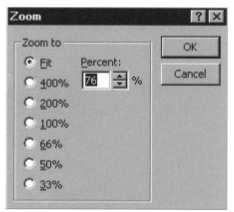

Click the radio buttons to select one of the other available zoom percentages to zoom in or out of a document. For example, if 200% is selected, the size of the slide would be double its actual size, and therefore be brought closer to you (zooming in) so you can only see a section of the slide on screen. By selecting 50%, the slide would appear half its actual size (zooming out). A common setting for working with slides is 75%, based on a 17" monitor size.

If a specific percentage is required which does not appear in the preset list, use the **Percent:** section to either type in the required percentage or use the up and down arrows to move in increments of 1% at a time.

Another method is to use the drop-down list of available ——————— zoom percentages from the Standard toolbar.

By selecting the **Fit** option, the entire slide will display in the PowerPoint Window.

T A S K	1.	*Open **PowerPoint** and open the existing presentation called **Introductory Presentation 2000** from your floppy disk.*
	2.	*View the presentation at **50%**, **66%**, **90%** and **200%**.*
	3.	*Finish on a suitable percentage setting (**50%**).*

Changing Slide Views

There are a number of ways to view your presentation within PowerPoint. Two of these are shown below:

Click on the slide view **Buttons** located at the bottom left of the screen

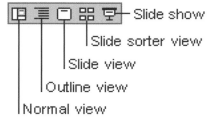

or

Click **View**.
Select a view option:

Normal View

Normal View contains three panes: the **Outline** pane, the **Slide** pane and the **Notes** pane. When using this view it allows working on all aspects of the presentation in one place. The size of the panes can be adjusted by clicking and holding the left mouse button on the pane borders.

Outline pane - Organise and develop the content of the presentation, add text and bullet points.

Slide pane - View how text looks on the slide and add graphics, movies, sounds and animation.

Notes pane - Add speaker notes or information to be shared with the audience.

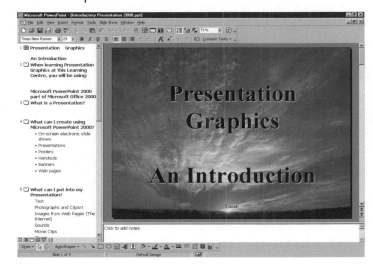

Outline View

Outline View gives a list of the titles and text in your presentation for easy editing and shows more than one slide at once. You can use the scroll bars to look down the list of slides. However, you cannot insert or edit graphics in this view. Outline view also gives you a small screen preview (called a thumbnail) of what the slide will look like. To select **Outline View**, click the **Outline View** button.

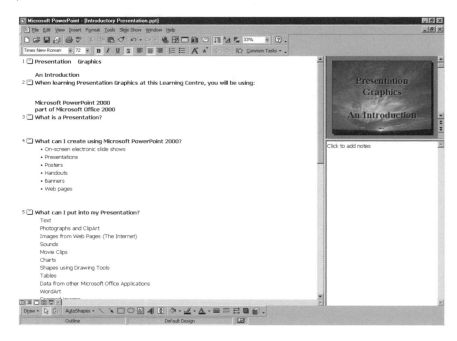

Slide View

Slide View shows one slide at a time. You can insert text, edit text, insert and edit images and graphics or draw shapes. Slide view is one of the most common views in PowerPoint. This is the view where your slides are both created and edited. To select **Slide View,** click the **Slide View** button.

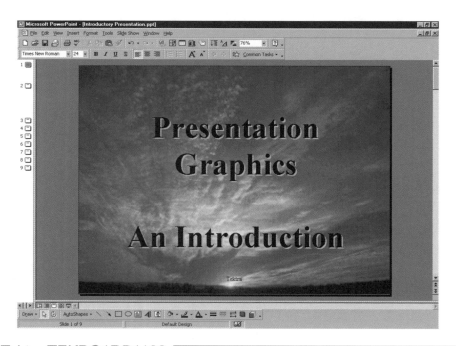

Slide Sorter View

Slide Sorter View is a slide summary, showing small preview screens of all slides contained in your presentation. The slides include text and graphics. This view is useful for changing the order of the slides, adding special effects and setting timings for electronic slide shows. To select **Slide Sorter View**, either click the **Slide Sorter View** button or select **View**, **Slide Sorter** from the menu bar.

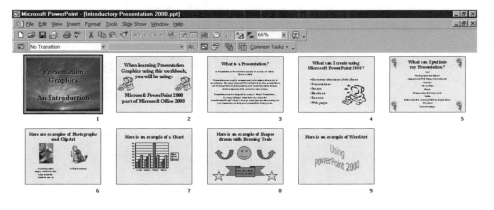

Notes Page View

Notes Page View shows miniatures of your slides, together with a section for notes. Notes can be printed so that you have a reference to key points in your presentation.

To select **Notes Page View**, select **View**, **Notes Page** from the menu bar.

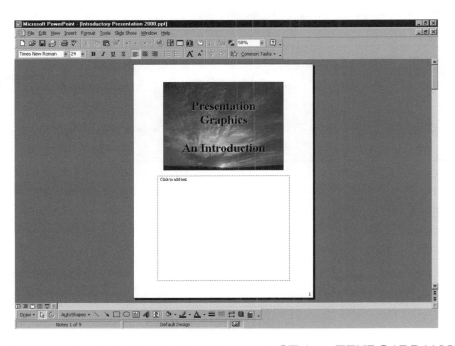

Slide Show View

Slide Show View will display your presentation as an electronic slide show and will appear in full screen mode. By clicking the left mouse button, you advance through the show (one slide at a time). Once the slide show reaches the last slide in the presentation, you are taken back to the view you were previously in.

To exit out of a slide show at any time, use the **Esc** key at the top left of the keyboard. Again, you will be taken back to the view you were previously in.

To select **Slide Show View**, either click the **Slide Show View** button or select **View**, **Slide Show** from the menu bar.

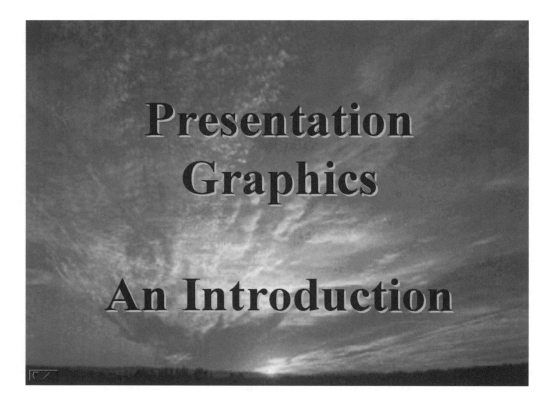

T A S K	1.	*View the presentation in Normal View, Outline View, Slide View, Slide Sorter View and as a Slide Show.*
	2.	*Save the presentation as **Introduction V2** to your floppy disk.*

Moving Around The PowerPoint Screen

By using the **Ctrl** key in conjunction with other keys, you can perform actions that you use regularly. The **Ctrl** keys are located on the keyboard. When using these keys, you are using a **shortcut**.

The Ctrl key:

Action	Keyboard Shortcut
To move to the first slide	**Ctrl+Home**
To move to the last slide	**Ctrl+End**
To move to the next slide	**Page Down (PgUp)**
To move to the previous slide	**Page Up (PgDn)**

Using the scroll bars to navigate around your presentation

An alternative is to use the vertical scroll bar and the horizontal scroll bar, by using the arrows at the top and bottom, left and right.

You can also use the following buttons on the vertical scroll bar, which are located at the bottom right of the PowerPoint window:

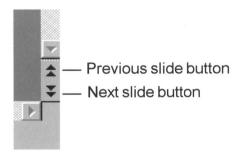

— Previous slide button
— Next slide button

T A S K	1.	*Use the above shortcuts to navigate through the presentation.*
	2.	*View slide 1 of the presentation in normal view.*

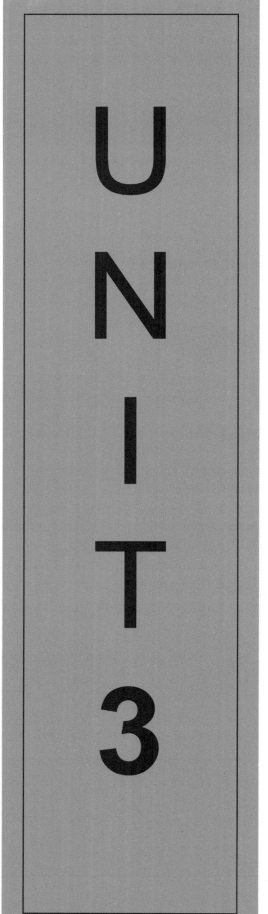

On completion of this unit you will have learnt about and practised the following:

- **Using Page Setup**

- **Printing Presentations**

  - Enabling Faster Printing And To Print In Black And White
  - Troubleshooting Printing Problems
  - Printing Slides In Greyscale or Black And White
  - Printing Options
  - Printer Properties

- **Using The Ruler**

- **Using The Guides**

Using Page Setup

Page Setup is used to set up and size a presentation to suit specific requirements depending on how it will be communicated to your audience. Options include sizing the presentation for an On-screen Show, A4 paper, Overheads and Banners. Presentation orientation is also set using the Page Setup option. This is how the presentation will be displayed (ie in landscape or portrait format). **Page Setup** should be used before printing a presentation to ensure it has been sized correctly for the type of output being used.

Click **File**, **Page Setup** to view the following dialogue box (Fig 6).

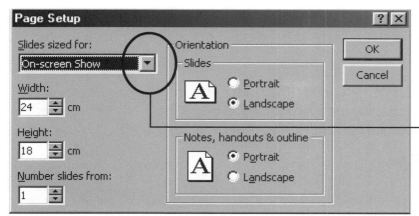

Fig 6

Click on the drop-down arrow to view the size options

By selecting the size required, the width and height measurements will change accordingly.

Presentations can be changed in orientation, depending on requirements. This can be landscape or portrait, but remember that monitors are in landscape format.

Landscape: Text will appear with the long edge of the paper at the top.

Portrait: Text will appear with the short edge of the paper at the top.

T A S K

1. *Ensure you are working on the **Introduction V2** presentation.*

2. *Size the presentation for A4 paper in landscape format.*

3. *Save the changes to the presentation.*

Printing Presentations

To produce a hard copy of your presentation, it will need to be printed. Ensure you are connected to a printer and it is loaded with paper and 'on-line' ready to print. Remember, if you are printing a presentation or slide which includes colour and you are printing to a monochrome (black and white) printer, the colour will not display.

Use either of the following methods to produce a print of your presentation:

Click on the **Print** icon on the Standard toolbar; the whole presentation will be printed.

The Print icon (above) is a quick way to print **ALL** of your presentation, but should not be used if you only require certain slides in the presentation or the presentation printed in a different way.

To set specific requirements for printing, click **File** from the menu bar, then click **Print**. This will display the **Print** dialogue box. See over the page for a description of this box (Fig 7).

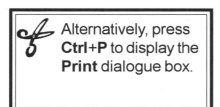

Alternatively, press **Ctrl+P** to display the **Print** dialogue box.

Options for printing your presentation include the following:

Slides   Print the slides as they appear on the screen.

Handouts   Printing handouts is useful for your audience to take away at the end of a presentation. Options include 2, 3, 4, 6 or 9 slides per page.

Notes Pages   Notes pages will show a miniature of the slide with notes underneath. Notes pages can be used by the speaker as prompts or reminders of certain stories or anecdotes to tell the audience as the show is presented.

Outline View   Printing a presentation in outline view is useful if you require a printout of the text only.

The **Print** Dialogue Box (Fig 7).

The Printer section displays the name of the printer you are connected to

The Print Range section enables you to print the whole presentation, the current slide or specific slides

The Print what: section allows you to select what to print, ie Slides, Handouts, Notes Pages or Outline View

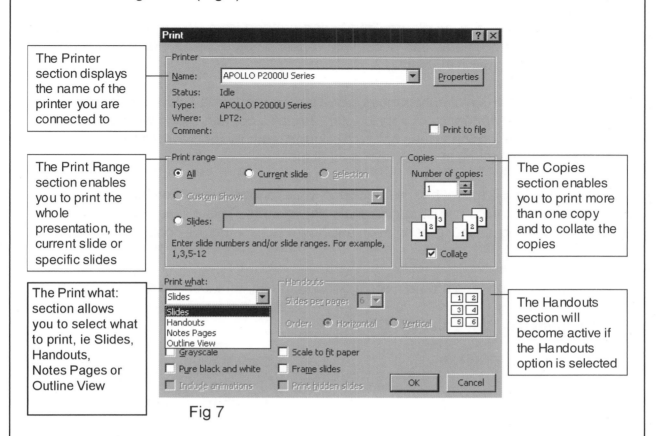

The Copies section enables you to print more than one copy and to collate the copies

The Handouts section will become active if the Handouts option is selected

Fig 7

NB   Screen pictures and stated selections may appear different to those stated, depending upon the printer installed.

Enabling Faster Printing And To Print In Black And White

When printing colour slides and presentations to a monochrome printer (black and white), you may experience problems such as the amount of time it takes to print a presentation. To overcome this, use the following procedure to enable faster printing and to set the printer to print in black and white.   Use of these procedures will depend on the type of printer being used.

Click **File** from the menu bar, click **Print**.

The dialogue box will appear as in Fig 7 above.   Click on the **Properties** button - this shows the print quality.

In the **Print what** section of the print dialogue box, locate the option for **Pure black and white.**   Select this option and ensure all other settings are correct.   Click **OK** to proceed with the print.

The settings above will be saved for the presentation you have open at the time, not for all future presentations.   Remember to use the settings in all presentations.

Troubleshooting Printing Problems

You may have access to a colour printer when printing from PowerPoint 2000, but be aware that certain problems can occur with regard to the colours viewed on screen in comparison with those on the print out.

Be aware that, in certain circumstances, large colour images can slow printing down; this will depend on the capability of your printer. Printers contain their own memory as do computers and if the printer does not hold enough memory for the image/slide to print, it may take a very long time to print or not print at all.

If you are printing to a monochrome (black and white) printer, the printer can only attempt to print coloured graphics by using greyscale conversion. This will again depend on the graphics appearing on your presentation and how much memory is contained in the printer being used.

To rectify possible printing problems on monochrome printers, use the following methods:

Preview Slides in Black and White

Use one of the methods below:

*   To preview in greyscale, click on the **Grayscale Preview** button on the Standard toolbar.

*   To preview in black and white, hold down the **Shift** key and click on the **Pure Black and White Preview** button on the Standard toolbar.

Printing Slides In Greyscale Or Black And White

Click on **File**, **Print** from the menu bar, and either:

*   Select the **Grayscale** check box to print in greyscale

*   Or, to hide all shades of grey and print in black and white, select the **Pure black and white** check box.

Printing Options

As PowerPoint has various output options including 35mm slides and transparencies etc, it is advisable to be familiar with the printer options available to you.

Before printing any slide show or presentation you must ensure that the correct settings have been selected in both the **Page Setup** dialogue box and the **Print** dialogue box.

The **Page Setup** dialogue box will allow you to select the type of output required:

When the drop-down menu has been selected you can select one of the options available. The slides will be sized according to the option selected.

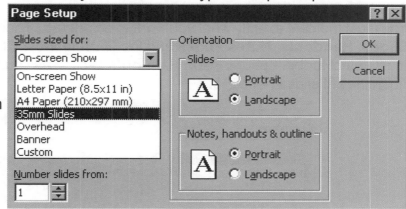

Use **Page Setup** before you add any object to a slide in your presentation, this will enable you to use the correct settings, sizes and measurements.

When you are ready to produce an output such as a paper print or transparencies, activate the **Print** dialogue box and select the output options.

If you are printing to a monochrome printer (black and white) it is vitally important (as previously discussed) that you select either **Grayscale** or **Pure black and white** when printing colour slides. Your presentation will print far quicker than if you try to print in colour when there is no capability to do this.

Familiarise yourself with the options in the **Print** dialogue box, be aware of the different settings.

Print range

Ask yourself which slides or how many slides you wish to print. You have the option to print the current slide, all slides or selected slides from a presentation.

In the example below a specific range of slides to print has been entered ie slides 2 to 6. The word 'to' is represented by the dash (-).

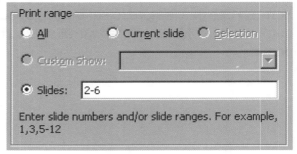

Copies

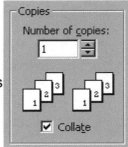

The **Copies** option is used like a photocopier; instead of printing one slide or one whole copy of the presentation and copying using a separate piece of equipment, you can produce all the required copies here. If you choose to collate them they will be printed in group order, ie 5 sets of slides 2-6.

Print what

You must indicate exactly what you want to be printed. There are options such as **Slides**, **Handouts**, **Notes Pages** and the **Outline View**. If you select **Handouts** you must select further options in the **Handouts** section as you can choose to print various quantities of slides per page.

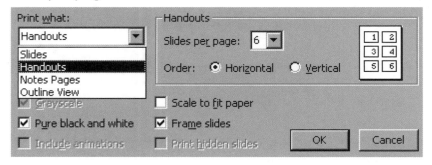

Notice the checkboxes entitled **Grayscale** and **Pure black and white** (as discussed previously); ensure one of these options is checked when printing to a black and white printer.

Printer Properties

All printers are installed with their own set of properties. Properties include the type of printer, quality (dpi), features (ie two page printing, orientation etc) and colour capabilities. Some printers may contain other options.

Clicking on the **Properties** button in the **Print** dialogue box will activate the properties of a printer:

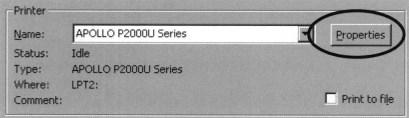

You can use this feature to set particular colour preferences for this printer or choose the output quality. Most printers will allow you to print in draft and in a higher quality for final printing.

**T
A
S
K**

1. Print the current presentation using the following criteria:

   Handouts
   9 per page
   Pure black and white

2. Print the current presentation using the following criteria:

   Outline View
   Grayscale

3. Preview the presentation in greyscale in Slide Sorter View.

4. Preview the presentation in colour in Slide Sorter View.

5. View the properties for the printer you are using. Note down the name of the printer and the quality setting currently being used.

6. Save any changes to the presentation.

Using The Ruler

Like word processing using Microsoft Word, Microsoft PowerPoint 2000 has a facility for aligning text and graphics. This is called the **Ruler** and there are horizontal and vertical rulers. Rulers can be displayed in centimetres (cm) or inches ("), but for PowerPoint 2000 it is recommended to work in cm. Measurement units are changed in the settings of the computer.

NB If the ruler is not showing, click **View** from the menu bar, click **Ruler**.

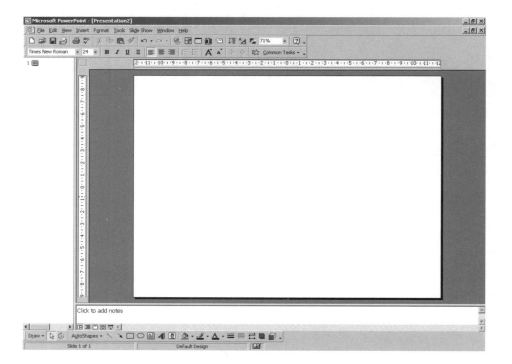

Rulers appear in Normal View, Slide View and Notes Page View, horizontally and vertically if selected.

Notice that the ruler has 'Zero' in the centre of both rulers. By moving the mouse over the slide without clicking, a position can be pinpointed. For example, to place a piece of text or graphic in the very centre of the slide, the two 'zero' co-ordinates on both rulers can be pinpointed.

Your ruler will look different depending on the percentage of 'zoom' set. Using zoom only affects what can be viewed on the current slide. This does not affect printing.

Using Guides

When aligning text or graphics on a slide, it may be necessary to align them into a specific position.

To help with this, PowerPoint has a facility called **Guides**, which is a cross-dashed line on the slide showing where the centre of the slide is.

To show guides, select **View** from the menu bar, click **Guides**.

When learning Presentation Graphics using this workbook, you will be using:

─── Horizontal guide

Microsoft PowerPoint 2000 part of Microsoft Office 2000

Vertical guide

Guides automatically appear to pinpoint the centre of the slide, but this can be altered by clicking and holding down the left mouse button and dragging into the required position. You can move one guide at a time, either the vertical or horizontal guide.

Guides can be duplicated, as there may be a need to align several objects. To duplicate a guide, click and hold the guide with the left mouse button, hold down the **Ctrl** key on the keyboard and drag the guide. By releasing the mouse button, a duplicate guide will appear.

To delete duplicated guides, click and hold the guide with the left mouse button and drag off the slide.

To turn off the ruler and the guides, click on **View**, **Ruler** and/or **View**, **Guides**.

T A S K	1.	*View the ruler for the presentation* **Introduction V2**.
	2.	*View the guides.*
	3.	*Save any changes and close the presentation.*

CONSOLIDATION EXERCISE

1. Open the existing presentation called **Introductory Presentation 2000**.

2. View the presentation as a slide show.

3. View slide 4 in notes page view.

4. View the presentation in outline view.

5. View the presentation in slide sorter view and amend the zoom setting to 100% and 90%.

6. View the presentation in normal or slide view.

7. Access the **Help** facility and search for help on **Working in Different Views**. Display the information regarding **PowerPoint Views**.

8. Close the **Help** window.

9. Size the presentation for 35mm slides in landscape format.

10. View the slide show.

11. View the presentation in normal view.

12. View the ruler and guides.

13. Duplicate the vertical guide until you have 4 guides.

14. Print slide 4 of the presentation in notes page format and in black and white.

15. Save any changes.

16. Close the presentation.

17. Close PowerPoint.

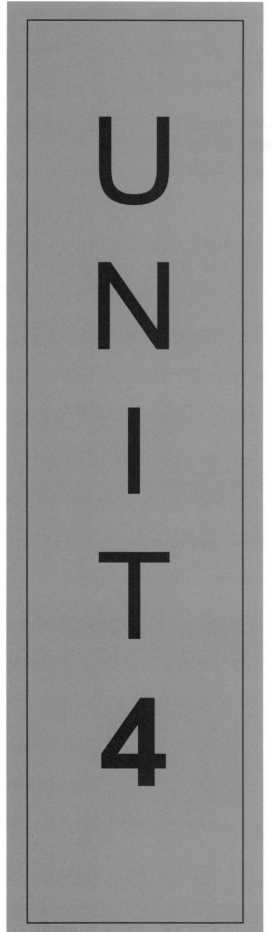

On completion of this unit you will have learnt about and practised the following:

- **Working With Text**

  - Adding And Working With Text
  - Keys For Moving Around In Text
  - Repositioning Text
  - Aligning Text
  - Line Spacing
  - Changing Case
  - Applying Attributes To Text
  - Formatting Text Placeholders And Text Boxes

Working With Text

Adding And Working With Text

Text can be added to a slide in the following ways:

- Using text placeholders in an AutoLayout
- Inserting a text box via the menu bar or the Drawing toolbar
- Inserting text directly via Outline View

Placeholders

A placeholder is a boxed area on the slide where text, graphics, charts, tables, Clip Art or objects can be added.

This is a **Text Placeholder:**

Click to add title

Notice the **selection handles** around the edges of the placeholder.

By clicking into the existing text with the left mouse button, your choice of text can be added to replace the existing words.

To de-select a placeholder, click anywhere outside the box with the left mouse button.

Inserting a text box via the menu bar and the drawing toolbar

Text can be added to a blank presentation, an AutoLayout, or even an existing presentation by inserting a text box.

To insert a text box via the menu bar:

Click **Insert, Text Box**.

The mouse pointer will change.

Indicate where the text box is to be inserted on the screen. Click, hold the left mouse button and drag a box shape.

Alternatively, click once and let go of the button and a text box will be created.

This will be small in size, but expands when text is inserted.

If a text box is not required, and nothing has been typed into it, click anywhere with the left mouse button outside of the box and it will disappear.

If the text box is no longer required and text has been typed into the box, select the box and press the **Delete** button on the keyboard.

To Insert a text box via the Drawing toolbar:

Click on the **Insert Text Box** button following the previous instructions to create the text box.

T A S K

1. Open **Microsoft PowerPoint**.

2. Open the existing presentation **Project V1**.

3. Navigate to slide view and add the title **Business Proposals 2002**.

4. Add the sub-title **A Presentation by** [**your name**] [**today's date**].

5. Save the changes to the presentation.

Formatting Fonts And Font Sizes

Fonts

A font is the character style of typeface. There are many different types of font available in PowerPoint 2000. To format the font of a piece of text, first highlight the selected text and select the font style required.

Click with the left mouse button on the drop-down arrow to view the fonts available.

Notice that the text has been highlighted.

Use the scroll bar to view other available fonts.

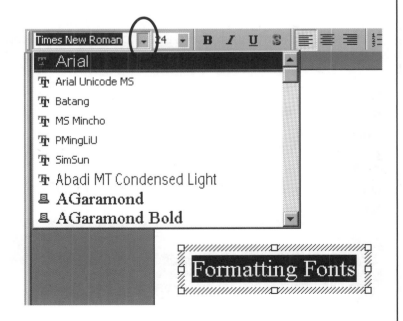

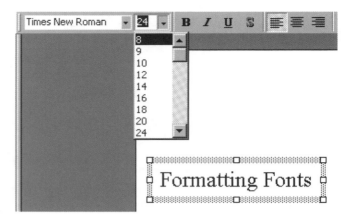

Change the size of the text using a similar procedure to changing the font.

Highlight the text then click the drop-down arrow on the Formatting toolbar to reveal the drop-down box:

An alternative way to change the font attributes is to use the menu bar after text has been highlighted.

Select **Format** from the menu bar, click **Font** and the following dialogue box will appear (Fig 8).

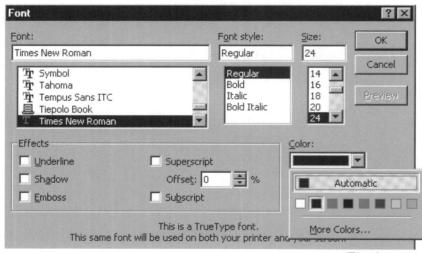

Select the **Font**, **Font style** and **Size** required, apply any effect and change the colour of text using this dialogue box.

Click **OK** to apply or **Cancel** to abandon.

Fig 8

Point size

Point size is the measurement used for character height. The larger the point size, the larger the text. A common size used for titles in PowerPoint 2000 is 44 points (pts).

T A S K		
	1.	*Format the title font to Tahoma size 48pt.*
	2.	*Format the sub-title font to Tahoma size 40pt.*
	3.	*View the presentation in outline view.*
	4.	*Size the presentation for an on-screen show in landscape format.*
	5.	*Print slide 1 in black and white and save the changes.*

<u>Selecting Parts Of Text In A Placeholder Or Text Box</u>

To use the mouse to select part of the text, click and drag over the text with the left mouse button.

Selecting Text with the mouse

To use the keyboard to select part of the text. Hover the mouse pointer in a suitable position and click the left mouse button.

To Select	Press
One character to the right	Shift+Right Arrow
One character to the left	Shift+Left Arrow
To the end of a word	Ctrl+Shift+Left Arrow
To the beginning of a word	Ctrl+Shift+Left Arrow
One line up	Shift+Up Arrow
One line down	Shift+Down Arrow

<u>Keys For Moving Around In Text</u>

To Move	Press
One character to the left	Left Arrow
One character to the right	Right Arrow
One line up	Up Arrow
One line down	Down Arrow
One word to the left	Ctrl+Left Arrow
One word to the right	Ctrl+Right Arrow
To the end of a line	End
To the beginning of a line	Home
Up one paragraph	Ctrl+Up Arrow
Down one paragraph	Ctrl+Down Arrow
To the end of a text box	Ctrl+End
To the beginning of a text box	Ctrl+Home
To the next title or body text placeholder	Ctrl+Enter

Repositioning Text

Once text has been inserted into either a text box or text placeholder, it can be placed anywhere on the slide.

To move, it will need to be selected (click once inside the text to display the selection handles).

By pointing the mouse
at the edge of the text
box, the mouse pointer
will change.

Depending on where you point, the mouse pointer can change in various ways:

↕   Extend the box vertically

↔   Extend the box horizontally

     Extend the box diagonally to the left*

     Extend the box diagonally to the right*

⬌   Reposition or move the box on the slide

Selection
handles _____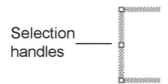

Depending on which selection handle is used.

Once the mouse pointer changes to any of the above symbols, click and hold the mouse button and drag to the required position.

TASK

1. *Navigate back to slide view.*

2. *Ensure the ruler and guides are displayed.*

3. *Position the horizontal guide at 0.00 and the vertical guide at 5 cm (left of centre).*

4. *Position the sub-title placeholder against the guides so that the left edge aligns against the vertical guide.*

5. *Save the changes.*

Aligning Text

There are four types of alignment available; left, centre, right and justify. They are used to align text within a placeholder or text box. (By default all text contained in a Title Text placeholder will align centre.) However, other types of alignment can be applied using the formatting toolbar. See below for an example of text with each different type of alignment applied.

Here at Clifton we have created a sanctuary especially for wildlife which have been injured or in danger.

Left alignment

To apply, select **Format**, **Alignment**, **Left** or use the button on the toolbar.

Here at Clifton we have created a sanctuary especially for wildlife which have been injured or in danger.

Centre alignment

To apply, select **Format**, **Alignment**, **Centre** or use the button on the toolbar.

Here at Clifton we have created a sanctuary especially for wildlife which have been injured or in danger.

Right alignment

To apply, select **Format**, **Alignment**, **Right** or use the button on the toolbar.

Here at Clifton we have created a sanctuary especially for wildlife which have been injured or in danger.

Justify

To apply, select **Format**, **Alignment**, **Justify**. The **Justify** button may not appear by default on your toolbar.

 Alternatively, use the following shortcuts:
Ctrl+L to left align
Ctrl+E to centre
Ctrl+R to right align
Ctrl+J to justify

TASK

1. *Format the sub-title text to appear centred.*

2. *Add a text box and position in the bottom left corner of the slide, add the text **Personnel Department V1**.*

3. *Format the text to match the existing fonts and format the size to 14pt.*

Line Spacing

When entering paragraphs of text within a slide, it may be necessary to adjust the line spacing. Spacing can be applied before a paragraph, after a paragraph or between the lines. Spacing is measured in either 'lines' or 'points'.

To format the line spacing of a paragraph, click anywhere in the paragraph which requires formatting, then select **Format** from the menu bar and click **Line Spacing**.

The **Line Spacing** dialogue box will appear:

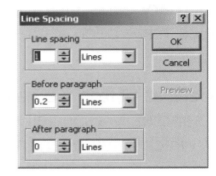

It is split into three sections; **Line spacing, Before paragraph** and **After paragraph**.

There are two options within each section, one to select the measurement value and one to select the measurement type, either lines or points.

Alternatively, a fast way to apply spacing in a paragraph is to use the **Increase spacing** and **Decrease spacing** buttons on the Formatting toolbar (if available).

Changing Case

The case of a character is whether it is a capital (uppercase) or not (lowercase). PowerPoint has a built-in feature which can change the case of typed text for you.

To change the case of characters, select the text, text box or placeholder and choose **Format** from the menu bar, then click **Change Case** and the following dialogue box will appear:

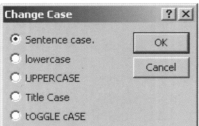

Notice that each option available gives an example of how the characters will look once changed. As with other dialogue boxes, click **OK** to confirm the changes or **Cancel** to abandon.

T A S K

1. *Format the line spacing of the sub-title text placeholder to 1.5.*

2. *Change the case of the text box in the bottom left corner to uppercase.*

3. *Save the changes.*

Applying Attributes To Text

Applying attributes to text includes formatting the text font. There are many different options available in **Format**, **Font** such as applying bold, underline, shadow and embossing. Other features include formatting the font colour and applying superscript and subscript. Here are some examples of these types of formatting:

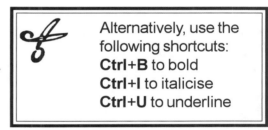

Bold   Shadow   Emboss

<u>Underline</u>   *Italics*

Superscript 200m^2 Subscript H$_2$O

Some of the most commonly used formatting options appear on the formatting toolbar. Remember that if you are not sure of a button's function, a 'tooltip' will appear after a few seconds of pointing the mouse pointer at the button to tell you what it is.

Alternatively, use the following shortcuts:
Ctrl+B to bold
Ctrl+I to italicise
Ctrl+U to underline

To use the other formatting options that are not available on the toolbar, select the text, text box or placeholder. Choose **Format**, **Font** from the menu bar.

The **Font** dialogue will be displayed:

Font, **Font style**, **Size**, **Effects** and **Color** can be altered from here. Make your selection and click **OK**.

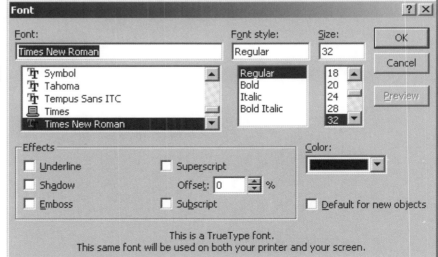

Adding colour to the presentation document will make it stand out and appear far more eye-catching than black and white. However, for printing purposes, black and white is far more economical.

To change the font colour, highlight or select the text requiring colour then select **Format**, **Font** and locate the drop-down arrow to reveal the colour palette.

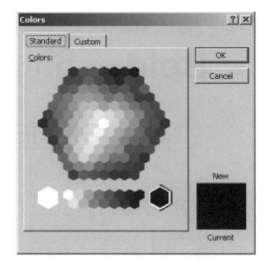

By selecting **More Colors**, the **Colors** dialogue box will appear.

This will give a wider range of choice. Click to select a colour, then click **OK** to confirm the choice or **Cancel** to abandon.

T A S K		
	1.	Apply bold to the title.
	2.	Apply italics to the text in the text box positioned in the bottom left corner of the slide and format the colour of the font to red.
	3.	Save the changes.

Formatting Text Placeholders And Text Boxes

Placeholders and text boxes can be formatted to include a lined border of various colours, thicknesses (weights) and styles. Fill colours can also be applied to make them stand out from the other objects within a slide.

If formatting a placeholder, select **Format** from the menu bar, then click **Placeholder**. If formatting a text box, select **Format** and **Text Box** (Fig 9). The following dialogue box will appear:

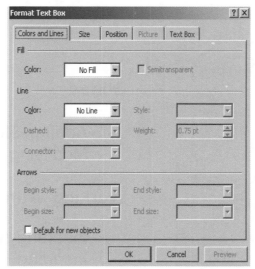
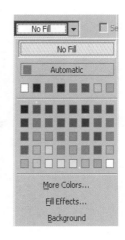

Fig 9

Notice the **Colors and Lines** tab. At present there is no **Fill Color** or **Line** applied to this text box. By clicking the drop-down arrow, further options can be selected. Select the **Text Box** (Fig 10) tab. The following options appear:

Fig 10

If a line of text reaches the edge of a text box, word wrap automatically wraps text onto the next line.

By selecting the resize option, the text box will automatically adjust to fit the text.

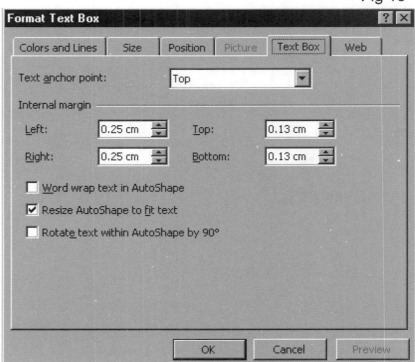

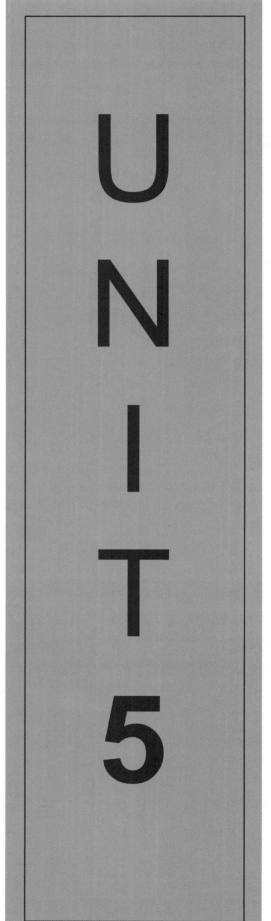

On completion of this unit you will have learnt about and practised the following:

- **Slides**

  - Adding Slides
  - Modifying The Slide Layout

- **Working With Bulleted Lists**

  - Inserting A Bulleted List
  - Inserting 2nd And 3rd Level Bullet Points

Slides

Adding Slides

A presentation can contain multiple slides. Add a slide by using either of the following methods using the menu bar, the Standard toolbar or the Common Tasks toolbar.

To add a slide using the menu bar, select **Insert**, **New Slide**. The **New Slide** dialogue box will then appear. Select the required **AutoLayout** for the new slide and click **OK**.

To add a slide using the Standard toolbar or Common Tasks toolbar, click on the **New Slide** button. The **New Slide** dialogue box will appear. Choose an **AutoLayout**.

> Alternatively, press **Ctrl+M** for a new slide.

Modifying The Slide Layout

It is possible to amend the slide layout (AutoLayout) of a slide. For example, if amending an existing slide and adding components such as a bulleted list, the layout can be updated to include a bulleted list placeholder.

To amend the layout, select **Format** from the menu bar, then click **Slide Layout**.

The **Slide Layout** dialogue box will appear, similar to the **New Slide** dialogue box but with slightly different wording. It will ask if you would like to reapply the current master style to the slide. If you are reapplying the same layout again, the button will remain as 'reapply'. If using a different layout, the button will change to **Apply**.

T A S K		
	1.	*Ensure you are working on the **Project V1** presentation.*
	2.	*Apply a light yellow fill colour to the Sub-title placeholder.*
	3.	*Apply a black line border around the Sub-title placeholder.*
	4.	*Add a new slide to make slide 2 and select the Bulleted List AutoLayout.*
	5.	*Add the title **Immediate Plans for 2002**.*
	6.	*Format the font to Tahoma, size 40pt, bold.*
	7.	*View the presentation in Outline View and Slide Sorter View.*

Working with Bulleted Lists

Inserting A Bulleted List

A bulleted list is a list of items with a bullet point to the left of each item. Bullets are 'markers' for the item. By default in PowerPoint, bullets will be displayed as small round black circles (unless the default has been changed).

There are many types of AutoLayout available for slides in a presentation. Several of these layouts contain bulleted list placeholders, making it easier to insert a bulleted list in a presentation.

Another method of applying bullets to a list is to use the bullet icon on the formatting toolbar. This acts as an on/off switch, ie, by highlighting a list of items and selecting the Bullet button, bullets will be applied (switched on), and by keeping the list highlighted and selecting the button again, bullets will be removed (switched off).

 The **Bullet** icon on the Formatting toolbar

A Bulleted List

- Monday
- Tuesday
- Wednesday
- Thursday
- Friday
- Saturday
- Sunday

T A S K

1. Ensure you are working on the **Project V1** presentation.

2. View slide 2 in Slide View.

3. Add the following text in Bulleted List format:

   Evaluate Staff Training Requirements
   Assess Staff Roles
   Personal Interview with all Staff
   Motivation Workshops Schedule

4. Format the font to match existing fonts and format to size 28pt.

5. Position the bulleted list placeholder 4cm from the left edge of the slide with the top edge of the placeholder 3cm above the horizontal centre line.

6. Print slide 2 in black and white.

7. Save and close the presentation.

Inserting 2nd And 3rd Level Bullet Points

It is possible to add 'levels' to bulleted lists. Levels are used where items displayed in a list have more information or data.

- # This is the First Level of a Bulleted List
  - Second level
    - Third level

You can work with bulleted lists using Normal, Outline or Slide View. However, when working with text, Outline View is particularly useful.

1 ☐ **Diary**
- Monday
- Tuesday
- Wednesday
- Thursday
- Friday

The example above indicates that we are working on slide 1, whose main title is Diary (in bold) and there is a bulleted list layout.

Adding additional items to the bulleted list

An additional line must be created to insert the additional text, therefore place the cursor at the end of the item before the additional line is to be created. In this example additional information is required for Tuesday. The cursor is placed at the end of the word **Tuesday**.

Press the **Return** key on the keyboard to create a blank line:

This will automatically create another bullet point with the same level as the one above.

1 ☐ **Diary**
- Monday
- Tuesday
- |
- Wednesday
- Thursday
- Friday

To change the bullet to a 2nd level bullet point press the **Demote** button on the Formatting toolbar.

Definitions of **Promote** and **Demote**:

Promote Making a point in a list stand out more than the line preceding it.

Demote ➡ Making a point in a list stand out less than the line preceding it.

By changing the bullet point type to a 2nd level bullet from a 1st level you are demoting the line of text.

To change it back you can either use the **Undo** button on the Standard toolbar or use the **Promote** button on the Formatting toolbar.

The demoted line of text appears here below the Tuesday item in the bulleted list. This makes it clear to the reader that the item relates to Tuesday.

1 ⬚ **Diary**
- Monday
- Tuesday
  - Advise Mr Parker of Interview
- Wednesday
- Thursday
- Friday

To add a further item below the Tuesday item, ensure the cursor is flashing at the end of the text 'Advise Mr Parker of Interview' and press **Return** to make a clear line.

A further 2nd level bullet point will appear.

To create a 3rd level bullet click on the **Demote** button once more.

This is an example of using 1st, 2nd and 3rd level bullet points in Outline View. This can be achieved in Slide and Normal View.

In cases of text being copied and pasted into Outline View, some further editing may be required. You may wish to try taking out all spaces that separate items and re-applying them (ie press **Return** again) to create the bullet point.

1 ⬚ **Diary**
- Monday
- Tuesday
  - Advise Mr Parker of Interview
    - Relevant files required
- Wednesday
- Thursday
- Friday

TASK

1. Start a new blank presentation using the Bulleted List AutoLayout.

2. View the presentation in Slide View and insert the bulleted list and title as shown below:

1 ⬚ **Weekly Schedule**
- Monday
  - Visit Mr Parker
  - Send off Form
- Tuesday
  - Telephone Mrs Simpson
    - Use Mobile Number
- Wednesday
- Thursday
- Friday
  - Play Golf with Roger
  - Dinner with Mary

TASK CONTINUED

3. *View the slide in Outline View.*

4. *Format the font of all bulleted text to Arial, size 24pt.*

5. *Format the title text to Arial, size 44pt, bold and centred.*

6. *Save the presentation as **Bullet Levels**.*

7. *Size the page for A4 paper in landscape orientation.*

8. *View the presentation in Slide View or Normal View, how does the display of text in the bulleted list differ with that in Outline View?*

9. *View the presentation in Outline View.*

10. *Place the cursor at the end of the item 'Dinner with Mary' and press **Enter** to create a new item.*

11. *Use the **Promote** button until this item becomes a new slide.*

12. *Add the New slide title **Reminders**.*

13. *Complete the items as shown in the example on the right.*

14. *Save the changes to the presentation.*

2 ☐ **Reminders**
- Take Wife to dinner
  - Her favourite restaurant
- Take the Dog to the Vet
  - Locate Vaccination forms
  - Book Booster
- Post off Tax Form
- Look in on Michael

15. *View the presentation in Slide View and format the placeholders as required.*

16. *Print the slides as handouts, 2 per page, in pure black and white.*

17. *Save any changes and close the presentation.*

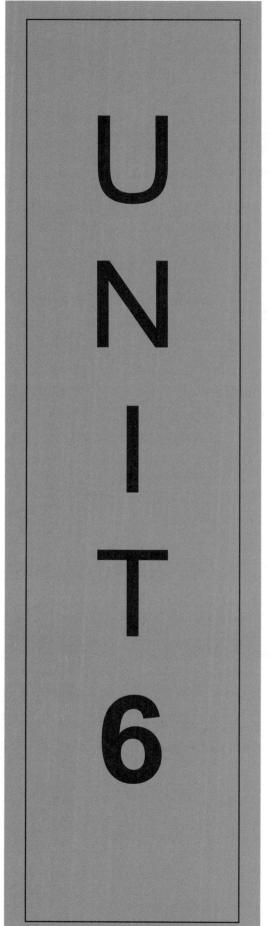

On completion of this unit you will have learnt about and practised the following:

- **Formatting Slide Backgrounds**

- **Working With Images**

  - Inserting Clip Art
  - Moving And Resizing Images
  - Inserting An Image From Disk
  - Inserting A Bitmap Image On A Slide
  - Saving A Paint File
  - Inserting A Paint Image Onto A Slide
  - Resizing Images Using Format Picture

Formatting Slide Backgrounds

To enhance the look of a presentation, the background of slides can be formatted to appear in various formats. These include colour, pattern and texture. Images can also be applied to slide backgrounds.

Fig 11

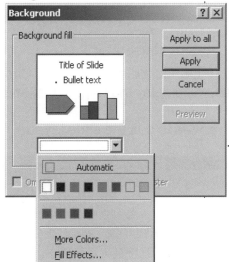

Select **Format** from the menu bar, click **Background**.

The **Background** dialogue box will appear (Fig 11).

Notice the drop-down list below the scheme layout. By clicking on the drop-down arrow, a selection can be made from colour palettes.

If your preferred colour does not appear, click on **More Colors** to display the standard colour palette. Make your selection and click **OK**.

The preview will show both the existing and the new background.

NB It is important to consider the background colour in relation to the colour of text in the presentation document. Applying a colour which is too dark may result in the text not being displayed clearly.

T A S K

1.   Open the presentation **Introduction V2**.

2.   Format the background of the whole presentation to a light blue and apply to all slides.

3.   View the presentation in Slide Sorter View and ensure all fonts stand out against the new background.

4.   Save the changes to the presentation.

5.   Close the presentation.

Working with Images

Inserting Clip Art

Microsoft PowerPoint has a built-in feature called the 'Clip Art Gallery', which is a library of images. To make a presentation document more powerful, images can be inserted which relate to the type of presentation being created, such as animal images for a presentation relating to a zoo or wildlife park.

To view the Microsoft Clip Art Gallery from within a slide, select **Insert**, **Picture**, **Clip Art** from the menu bar or use the **Clip Art** icon on the Drawing toolbar.

Alternatively, if creating a new slide, an AutoLayout which includes a placeholder for Clip Art is available, which, when double-clicked with the mouse, will display the Clip Art Gallery.

Once an image has been inserted, it can be resized and moved to suit the slide layout.

To display the Clip Art Gallery click on **Insert**, **Picture**, **Clip Art** (Fig 12).

A list of Clip Art categories are available.

To view images, click on the category name.

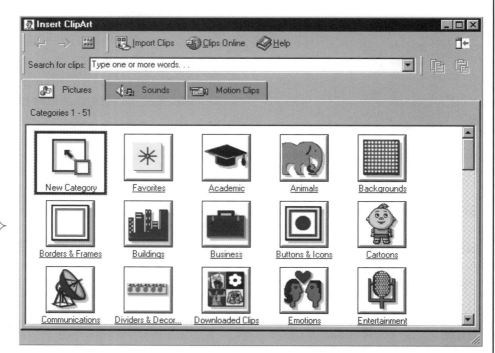

Fig 12

Click on an image to insert it and then select the **Insert** button from the menu.

The Clip Art Gallery will remain open.

Click on the close button when all required images have been inserted.

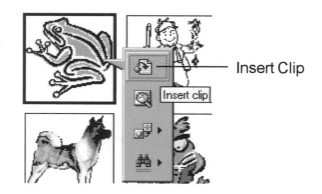

Insert Clip

Moving And Resizing Images

When an image has been inserted, it can be moved and resized to suit the layout of the slide.

Click once with the left mouse button to select the image and display the selection —— handles.

To move an image within a slide, point the mouse to the centre of the image until the mouse pointer changes to display the 'move' symbol.

Click and hold the left mouse button and drag to the required position on the slide. Release the mouse button when the position is reached.

Images have **selection handles** for resizing in the same way as placeholders and text boxes. By selecting the appropriate selection handle, the image can be made larger or smaller. To ensure the image stays in proportion, use the 'diagonal resize' handles and drag inwards or outwards holding the left mouse button down. Alternatively, hold down the **Shift** key whilst resizing.

T A S K

1. *Open the presentation called **Project V1**.*

2. *View slide 2 and add a new slide to make slide 3 using a placeholder which includes text and Clip Art.*

3. *Add the title **Possible Plans for 2002**.*

4. *Format the font to match previous titles.*

5. *Add a bulleted list to include the following points:*
    ***Relocation of Premises; Open Bristol Office; Open Leeds Office; Recruitment Drive; In-house training**.*

6. *Add a suitable Clip Art image to the slide and save changes.*

Inserting An Image From Disk

Having explored Clip Art and the Clip Art Gallery, there are other available options when inserting images or Clip Art into a presentation. An image or piece of Clip Art can be saved to disk, such as the floppy disk, as a file. There are other storage locations in which a piece of Clip Art can be obtained, such as a CD-ROM.

There are many CD-ROMs available containing thousands of images for use in this type of application. The Internet is also a useful resource for obtaining images depending upon the copyright implications.

To insert an image from floppy disk:

Click **Insert**, **Picture, From File,** from the menu bar.

The **Insert Picture** dialogue box will be displayed (Fig 13).

Change the **Look in:** box to read **3½ Floppy (A:)**

Fig 13

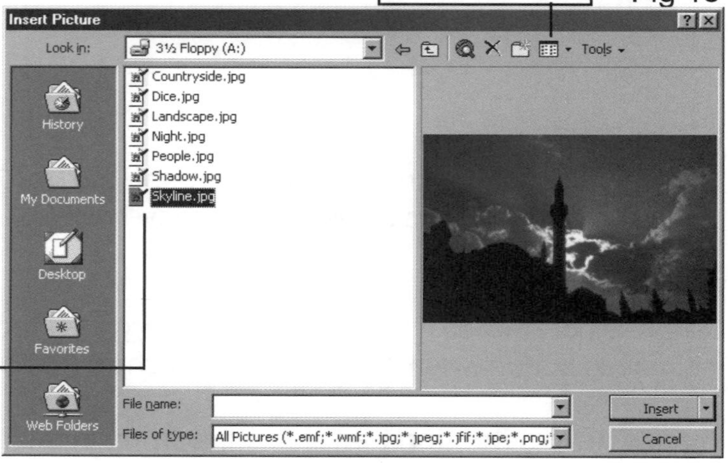

Select the image file required. A preview of the image may appear on the right, allowing you to view the image before inserting. If a preview does not appear, click on the **Views** button and select the **Preview** option.

Click **Insert** and the image will appear on the slide. Use the move handle or selection handles to reposition the image if required.

Image files are commonly used in presentation graphics applications and are available in various formats. This will depend on the resolution, quality and size of the graphic. To view the type of image file and its size, view the contents of the disk in Windows Explorer.

Listed below are some of the most common types of image files (file extensions) used in presentations:

.bmp   Bitmap image, available in a variety of formats. This format can display millions of colours.

.gif   Graphics Interchange Format, used on the World Wide Web, displays compressed image formats and therefore smaller file sizes. This format can also be animated (moving pictures).

.jpeg or .jpg   Developed by the Joint Photographic Experts Group and commonly used on the Web, this format is used for displaying high quality photographic images containing many colours.

Inserting A Bitmap Image Onto A Slide

Bitmap images are usually higher in file size as they have the capability of displaying millions of colours within the image resolution. Bitmap images can be created in an application called Paint. Paint is an integral part of the Microsoft Windows Operating System.

To start the Paint application, click on **Start**, **Programs**, **Accessories**, **Paint**.

The **Paint** window will display:

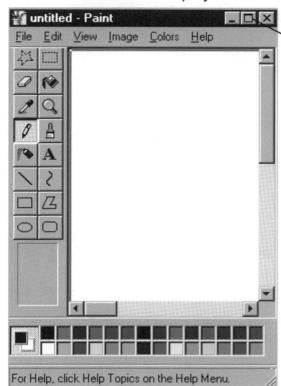

You can make the Paint window fill the whole screen by clicking on the **Maximise** button at the top right of the window if you prefer.

The Paint window consists of a toolbar and a palette of colours.

To view the function of each tool on the toolbar use the Screen Tip facility, ie rest the mouse pointer over a tool and after a few seconds the name of the tool will appear:

The Paint application is used to edit existing images by retouching or recolouring. It can also be used to create drawn objects. When a drawn object is created in Paint, it can be inserted as a file into any other Office application using the **Insert**, **Picture**, **From File** command on the menu bar.

The Paint toolbar

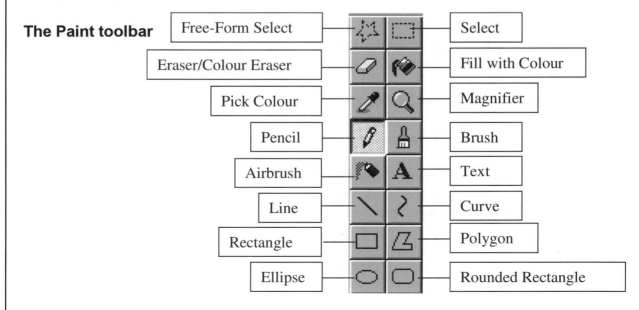

The toolbar is similar to the Drawing toolbar in PowerPoint, but there are more features, such as the **Airbrush** and **Eraser**.

To use any of the tools they must be activated on the toolbar. An activated tool will appear greyed out or sunken. In the above description of the toolbar the **Pencil** is selected.

When a tool has been activated and the mouse rested over the white work area of the screen the mouse pointer will change to accommodate the new command. For example, if the **Pencil** is selected, the mouse pointer changes to a symbol of a pencil in the white work area.

To draw on the white work area with the pencil, click and hold the left mouse button and drag to draw the required shape. Then release the mouse button.

In the example to the right, a picture of a face has been drawn using tools from the toolbar:

To change to a different colour, click to activate the required tool and then click on a colour from the palette. You can also select different size tools (eg pencils and brushes) once activated.

Saving A Paint File

To save an image drawn in Paint click on **File**, **Save** from the menu bar or **Ctrl+S**.

This will activate the **Save As** dialogue box and this works similar to other **Save As** dialogue boxes in other Microsoft applications.

Select a location to save in (ie **3½ Floppy (A:)**) from the drop-down list.

Type in a file name for the drawn image.

Click on the **File type** drop-down list and select a format to save in. You can select various bitmap resolutions; the higher the resolution, the higher the file will be in size. Alternatively, you can select jpeg image that is a compressed format and far lower in file size.

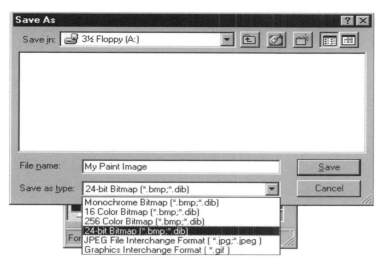

Click on the **Save** button when you have selected a type.

To close the Paint application, either click on **File**, **Exit** from the menu bar, press **Alt+F4** from the keyboard or use the cross in the top right corner.

Inserting A Paint Image Onto A Slide

To insert an image that has been created in the Paint application, use the same method as for inserting an image from disk.

View the slide where the image is to be placed.

Click on **Insert**, **Picture**, **From File**.

Select the location where the image is stored. Click on **Insert**.

The image will appear with selection handles that can be resized as necessary.

T A S K		
	1.	Start a new blank presentation using the blank AutoLayout.
	2.	Start the Paint application and view in full screen.
	3.	Draw an image of a tree using a large amount of the white space provided (the image can be resized when inserted onto a slide). You do not have to be too precise!
	4.	Save the image as a jpeg type file called **Tree**.
	5.	Close Paint.
	6.	Navigate back to the blank PowerPoint presentation and view slide 1 in Slide View.
	7.	Insert the image of the **Tree** and resize if necessary.
	8.	Save the presentation as **Tree** and close.

Resizing Images Using Format Picture

Resizing can be carried out using the selection handles appearing around the image or object when selected. However, an alternative way to resize images is to select the image and use **Format**, **Picture** from the menu bar.

The **Format Picture** dialogue box will be displayed (Fig 14):

Select the **Size** tab.

This will display the current height and width of the image.

Lock aspect ratio - when this box is selected, the ratio of the image will be maintained and will not appear distorted.

To resize any height and width measurements, click into the height and width boxes and retype the measurement required.

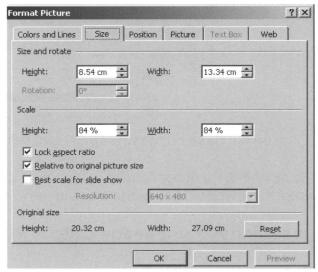

Fig 14

You do not have to enter the 'cm' for centimetres or an inches sign (") , as they will be inserted for you.

If any measurements are entered by mistake, click **Reset**. The picture will be reset to its original size and ratio.

When measurements have been changed, the scaling section will automatically adjust according to the best scale for the image.

T A S K		
	1.	*Ensure you are working on the presentation **Project V1**.*
	2.	*Click on slide 3 and add a new slide to make slide 4 selecting the **Title Slide** AutoLayout.*
	3.	*Add the title **Motivation Workshops** and format the font as previous titles.*
	4.	*Add the sub-title:* **Motivation workshops will commence in February 2002 by Outsource Ltd.**
	5.	*Format the sub-title font to Tahoma, size 32pt and centre align the text.*
	6.	*Add the image from the floppy disk called **Skyline.jpg** and position on the left and under the sub-title text. Resize the image to approximately 7cm high x 10cm wide.*
	7.	*Save the changes to the presentation.*

T A S K

1. Start a new blank presentation using the Blank AutoLayout.

2. Insert an image from the Clip Art Gallery.

3. Add a new slide using the Blank AutoLayout.

4. Insert an image from file onto slide 2 of the presentation.

5. View slide 1 of the presentation in Slide View.

6. Size the Slide Show for A4 paper in landscape orientation.

7. View the ruler and the guides.

8. Save the presentation as **Resizing Images**.

9. Position guides on slide 1 as follows:

    Vertical 9cm (left of centre)
    Horizontal 2cm (above centre)

10. Resize the Clip Art image to approximately 5cm high x 4cm wide.

11. Position the image with the left edge along the vertical guide and the bottom edge along the horizontal guide.

12. Move the horizontal guide to 1cm below centre.

13. Resize the image (maintaining proportion) using the selection handles so that the bottom edge of the image is aligned along the horizontal guide.

14. Save the changes to the presentation.

15. View slide 2 in Slide View.

16. Position the guides as follows:

    Vertical: 3cm (left of centre)
                     3cm (right of centre)

    Horizontal: 0cm (centre)

17. Resize the image so that the right and left edges of the image are aligned along the vertical guides.

18. Ensure the centre selection handles are aligned along the horizontal guide.

19. Save the changes to the presentation and close.

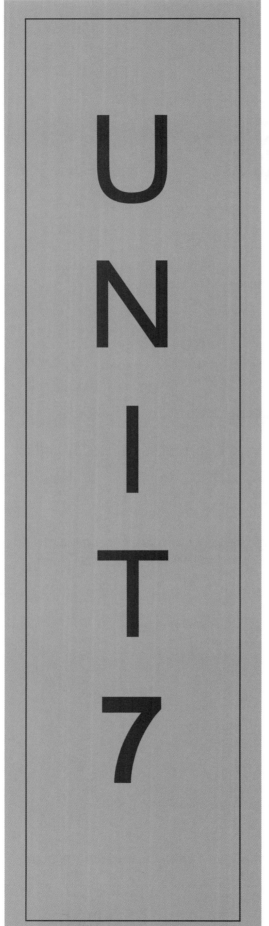

On completion of this unit you will have learnt about and practised the following:

- **Using Cut, Copy And Paste**

  - Using Cut, Copy And Paste With Text, Images And Slides

  - The Clipboard

- **Deleting Objects And Text**

Using Cut, Copy And Paste

Using Cut, Copy And Paste With Text, Images And Slides

Three useful tools within any of the Microsoft Office 2000 applications are **Cut**, **Copy** and **Paste**. Objects can be moved, copied and pasted to other locations within either the existing presentation, another presentation or another application.

Cut - To **move** an object, selected text, image, slide etc from one location to another (used in conjunction with paste).

Copy - To **duplicate** an object, selected text, image, slide etc to create a copy (used in conjunction with paste).

Paste - To complete either of the above actions.

> 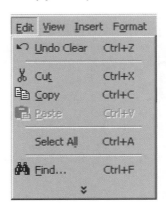 Alternatively, use the following shortcuts:
> **Ctrl+X** to cut
> **Ctrl+C** to copy
> **Ctrl+V** to paste

The standard procedure for cutting and copying:

1.   Select the object, text, image or slide.

2.   Click **Cut** (move) or **Copy** (duplicate).

3.   Selected item is placed on the **clipboard** (not visible).

4.   Select the required location and click **Paste**.

Use either of the following methods to access cut and paste **or** copy and paste.

Select **Edit**, **Cut** from the menu bar, followed by **Edit**, **Paste**.

Select **Edit**, **Copy** from the menu bar, followed by **Edit**, **Paste**.

or use the buttons on the Standard toolbar.

Cut   Copy   Paste

The Clipboard

The clipboard is an area of temporary memory which will hold data, whether cut or copied, for it to be pasted elsewhere.

When you copy an item, the original will stay in its original position, and a copy of it will be placed on the clipboard.

Cut, copy and paste can be used either within one slide or between slides. For example, if an image is required on slides 2, 5 and 10, the image can be copied (held on the clipboard) and pasted into slides 5 and 10. Once the application is closed, the clipboard will be emptied and its contents lost.

Cut, copy and paste can also be used between applications, as long as they are compatible with each other. For example, text can be cut or copied from a Word document and pasted into a presentation document.

Deleting Objects And Text

To delete an object such as a placeholder, text box or image, select the object and either select **Edit**, **Clear** from the menu bar or press the **Delete** key on the keyboard.

To delete text, highlight or select the section of text to be removed, and either select **Edit**, **Clear** from the menu bar or press the **Delete** key on the keyboard.

Remember that if you make a mistake and delete by accident, you can use the **Undo** button on the toolbar or select **Edit**, **Undo**, which will undo the last action carried out.

TASK

1. Ensure you are working on the **Project V1** presentation.

2. Add a new slide to make slide 5 and select a title only layout.

3. Copy the third bullet point from slide 2 into the title on slide 5 and make bold.

4. Insert a text box on the left-hand side of the slide under the title and add the following text:

    Roger Moran will hold personal interviews and staff are to provide feedback.

5. Copy the Clip Art image from slide 3 to the right-hand side of slide 5.

6. Delete the text stating **Open Leeds Office** on slide 3.

7. Save the changes and close the presentation.

CONSOLIDATION EXERCISE

1. Create a new blank presentation using the bulleted list AutoLayout for slide 1.

2. Size the presentation for an on-screen show in landscape format.

3. Format the background of the slide to a light green.

4. Add the title text **The United Kingdom**.

5. Format the title text for Arial, size 44pt and bold.

6. Format the title text placeholder to have a yellow fill colour and a black line border.

7. Add the bulleted list:

    England
    Scotland
    Wales
    Northern Ireland

8. Resize both placeholders to suit the text.

9. Add a new slide to make slide 2, select the bulleted list AutoLayout.

10. Format the background to match slide 1.

11. Add the title **Major Resources of the UK** and format the text to Arial size 36pt.

12. Add the following text in bulleted list format:

    Natural Gas; Oil; Coal; Iron/Steel; Agricultural Crops & Livestock; Fisheries; Tourism.

13. Format the font in a size to suit the slide layout.

14. Add a new slide to make slide 3 and select the title only AutoLayout.

15. Add the title **Physical Features**, format the font as before and add the image from floppy disk called **Countryside.jpg**.

16. Place the image in a suitable position on the slide and resize if necessary.

17. Print the presentation, save as **United Kingdom** and close.

25/8.

On completion of this unit you will have learnt about and practised the following:

- **Reordering Slides**

- **Duplicating Slides**

- **Deleting Slides**

- **Working With Drawn Objects**

  - Adding, Moving And Resizing Lines And Arrows
  - Add Text To A Pre-Defined Shape
  - Adding Text Directly Into An AutoShape
  - Formatting Objects
  - Formatting Arrows
  - Rotate And Flip

- **Grouping Text With Graphical Objects**

  - Grouping
  - Reposition And Resize Grouped Objects

- **Layering**

Reordering Slides

Once a presentation has been created, it may be necessary to amend the slide order. This task is carried out using Slide Sorter View, where all slides in the presentation can be viewed at once (depending on the zoom setting). Cut, copy and paste can be used in this view to amend the slide order.

To reorder slides, click on the **Slide Sorter** view button or select **View**, **Slide Sorter** from the menu bar.

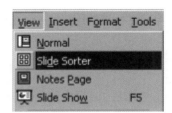

To select a slide, click once on the slide with the left mouse button. A border will appear around the edge of the slide selected.

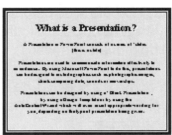

To amend the slide order:

1.   Select the slide which requires moving.

2.   Select **Edit**, **Cut** from the menu bar (or use the **Cut** tool on the toolbar).

3.   Select a new location for the slide (click the left mouse button in-between any of the existing slides a vertical line will appear). Click to the right of the last slide if it is to be placed at the end of the presentation.

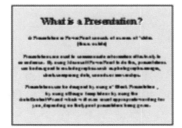
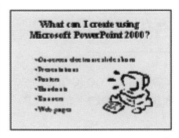

4.   Click on **Edit**, **Paste** from the menu bar or use the button on the toolbar.

The same can be achieved by using 'drag and drop'. Click and hold the slide to be moved with the left mouse button and 'drag' to the new position. Release the mouse once in position.

Duplicating Slides

Duplicating a slide is to make a copy of an existing slide. The advantage of duplicating slides in presentations means that any existing formatting on the slide will be copied over to the new slide automatically, reducing the need to format a new slide again. Any existing text can be replaced (typed over) with the new text, and any images or objects can be replaced with new ones.

To duplicate (make a copy of) a slide, either use **Copy** and **Paste** or use **Edit**, **Duplicate** from the menu bar.

Copy and **Paste** will allow you to specify the location in which to insert the duplicate slide before creating it. **Edit**, **Duplicate** will directly insert a duplicate to the right of the original slide, which can be moved afterwards.

To make a copy of a slide using copy and paste, select the slide, select **Edit**, **Copy** from the menu bar or use the copy button on the toolbar.

Select a new location as per the instructions above, and select **Edit**, **Paste** or use the button on the toolbar.

Note: If using copy and paste, you need not specify a location; simply select the slide, click **Copy** and then paste straight away. This is the same as selecting the slide and selecting **Edit**, **Duplicate** or **Insert, Duplicate Slide** from the menu bar.

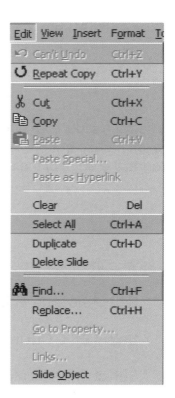

Deleting Slides

To delete a slide which is no longer required, whilst in Slide Sorter View, select the slide, and either press the **Delete** key on the keyboard, or select **Edit**, **Delete Slide** from the menu bar.

Edit, **Delete Slide** can also be used in **Slide View**, **Outline View** and **Notes Page View.**

Remember, you can use the **Undo** button if you delete the wrong slides.

 ©Tektra TEKPG1RP1102

T A S K

1. Open the presentation **Project V1**.

2. View in Slide Sorter View.

3. Amend the slide order so that slide 5 becomes slide 4.

4. Duplicate slide 3 to make slide 4 and change the title in slide 4 to **Evaluate Staff Training**.

5. Replace the text with a bulleted list to read:

   Marketing
   Finance
   I.T.
   Sales

6. Duplicate slide 4 to make slide 5.

7. Replace the title in slide 5 to read **Assess Staff Roles**.

8. Delete the bulleted placeholder and add a text box under the title.

9. Format the text box to Tahoma, size 32pt and enter the following text:

   Mark Dobson will be assessing current roles and responsibilities.

10. Print the presentation as handouts, 9 per page in black and white.

11. Save the presentation.

12. View the presentation.

13. Close the presentation.

Working With Drawn Objects

Using the drawing toolbar is an effective way to enhance a presentation. Objects such as lines, arrows and shapes can be created. The toolbar consists of a **Draw** menu and an **AutoShapes** menu. The **Draw** menu allows the use of tools such as rotate, flip, group and ungroup. The **AutoShapes** menu (as displayed below) contains shapes such as block arrows, callouts, stars and banners etc.

The Drawing toolbar:

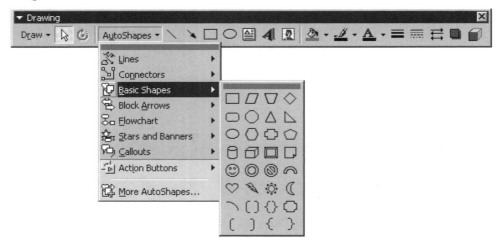

The drawing toolbar is usually located at the bottom of the PowerPoint window. If the toolbar is not displayed, click **View**, **Toolbars**, **Drawing**.

To draw an object on a slide:

1.   Select the object required, the 5-point star has been used in this example (from the **AutoShapes** menu).

2.   Point the mouse in the position where the object is required on the slide. The mouse pointer will change to a black cross to mark the position.

3.   Click with the left mouse button, hold and drag to the required size, release the mouse button.

4.   The shape will be created on the slide together with selection handles for moving and resizing the shape if required.

The shape will appear in the 'default' colour setting. This can be changed.

Formatting objects is covered later in this Unit.

As you can see there are many object types available. Once drawn, the objects can be formatted with different fill colours, line colours, rotated, flipped (turned upside down or mirrored), stretched and resized.

If you are unsure of the name of an object, point the mouse pointer at the shape button and wait approximately 1 second. The name will appear as illustrated.

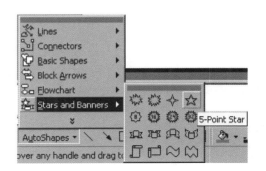

T A S K		
	1.	*Create a new blank presentation and select the title only AutoLayout.*
	2.	*View in slide view and add the title* **Project Plans**.
	3.	*Format the title font to Arial size 44pt in bold.*
	4.	*Using the drawing toolbar, draw the house as illustrated in Fig 15 below.*
	5.	*Format the background colour to light yellow.*
	6.	*Save the presentation as* **House**.
	7.	*Print slide 1.*

25/8.

Fig 15

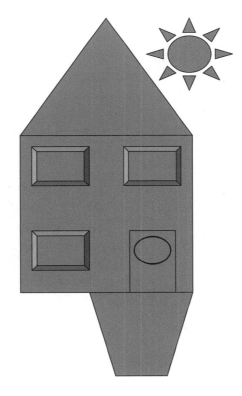

Adding, Moving And Resizing Lines And Arrows

Lines and arrows can be added to a slide using the same method as for adding shapes. Select the type of line or arrow required from the **AutoShapes** menu on the Drawing toolbar, then click and drag where the line or arrow is required. (The line or arrow can be drawn in at any angle or pointing in any direction).

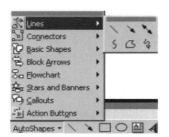

Alternatively, if a simple plain line is required, use the Line tool on the toolbar.

To move a line or arrow:

Move the mouse pointer over the line or arrow until the mouse pointer changes to the move handle symbol.

Click and hold the left mouse button and drag to the required position. On releasing the mouse button, the line or arrow is repositioned. The angle of the line or arrow can be changed by clicking on either of the end selection handles and dragging to the new angle.

To resize a line or arrow:

Click and hold the left mouse button over either of the end selection handles and drag to the required size. On release of the mouse button, the line is resized.

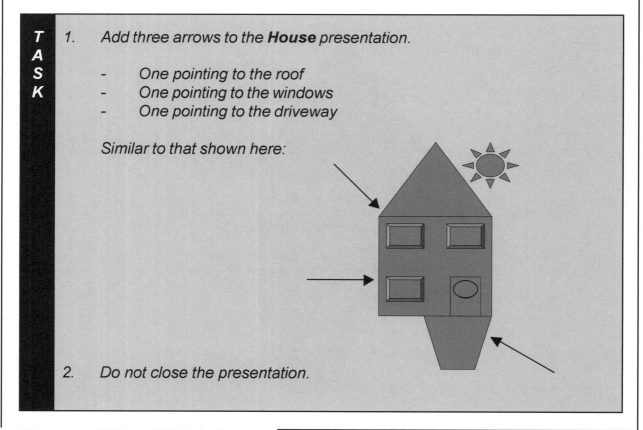

T
A
S
K

1. Add three arrows to the *House* presentation.

   - *One pointing to the roof*
   - *One pointing to the windows*
   - *One pointing to the driveway*

   Similar to that shown here:

2. *Do not close the presentation.*

Add Text To A Pre-Defined Shape

A pre-defined shape can be any of the AutoShapes from the Drawing toolbar. It may be necessary to add text to such shapes for creating logos etc. Text can be added using two methods: either create a text box and position it within (or on top of) the AutoShape or select the shape, click on the **Text box** tool on the Drawing toolbar and click on the shape.

Using a Text box and an AutoShape

Select an AutoShape from those available and resize as necessary.

Click on the **Text box** tool on the Drawing toolbar.

Draw the text box on the slide and type in the text required.

Reposition the text box to appear within the shape (see example below).

The example, left, shows an AutoShape of a callout that has been drawn and a text box placed separately. The text box has then been placed on top of the AutoShape so that the text appears within it.

When using this method, the text box can be formatted separately to have a different fill colour and borderline from the AutoShape appearing behind it.

Adding Text Directly Into An AutoShape

Select and draw the AutoShape on a slide and resize as necessary.

Click on the AutoShape to select it (ensure the selection handles appear).

Right-click with the right mouse button and select **Add Text**.

Enter the text as required.

Select the AutoShape, click on **Format**, **AutoShape** from the menu bar.

Select the **Text box** tab.

Format the shape to allow word wrap and resize to fit the text.

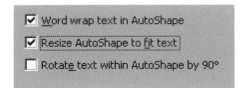

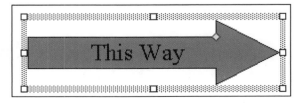

**T
A
S
K**

1.   Start a new blank presentation and select the blank AutoLayout.

2.   Create the drawn objects shown below (use guides if necessary):

Format the text to Arial, size 18pt.

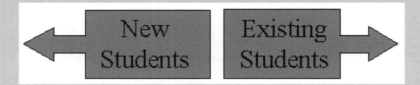

3.   Save the presentation as **Signs**.

4.   Print slide 1 in pure black and white.

5.   Close the presentation.

31/9.

Formatting Objects

As previously shown, objects drawn on a slide will appear in a 'default' colour. To customise the look of drawn objects use the **Format**, **AutoShape** command or use the tools available on the drawing toolbar. Objects can be changed in colour, border line colour, style and thickness.

If adding arrows to a slide, they can be changed to appear with a different arrowhead, thickness and style. This can either be carried out using the Drawing toolbar, or by selecting **Format**, **AutoShape** from the menu bar.

Ensure the object has been selected on the slide to indicate which shape is being worked with. The selection handles will appear around a selected object.

Click **Format**, **AutoShape** to display the dialogue box:

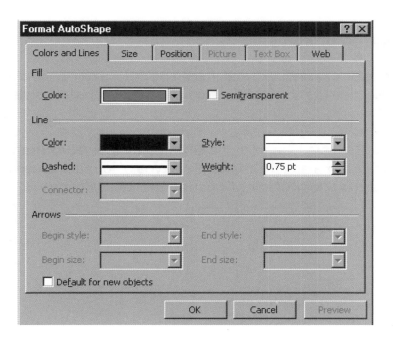

The dialogue box is split into three sections.

Fill - select a different fill colour for an object.

Line - select a different line colour, style and weight.

Arrows - select a different style for arrows or add arrowheads.

Formatting Arrows

Arrows can be inserted onto a slide using the Drawing toolbar, AutoShapes menu (Lines).

These options will add two basic arrow types, ie an arrow and a double arrow as shown below:

To format the style of the arrow, select the arrow so that the selection handles appear:

Select **Format**, **AutoShape** from the menu bar.

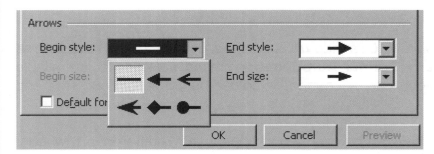

The **Arrows** section of the dialogue box will be activated.

Arrows can be formatted in **Begin style**, **Begin size**, **End style** and **End size**.

Click on each drop-down list in turn to view the options available.

To select the options click on **OK**.

Additionally a plain drawn line can be converted into an arrowhead at any time. Draw the line, and keep it selected (ensure the selection handles appear).

Click on **Format**, **AutoShape** from the menu bar.

The **Arrow** section of the dialogue box will indicate that the shape is a plain line. Click on the drop-down lists to make a selection (as above) for the begin style and the end style of the arrow.

The example below started as a Scribble Line from the Drawing toolbar **AutoShapes** menu and was then formatted to become an arrowhead. This type of formatting can be useful where you need to make arrows point at specific parts of a slide or image.

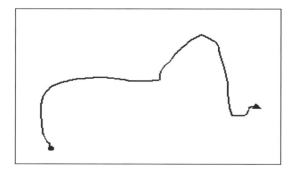

T **A** **S** **K**	1.	Using the **House** presentation, format the fill colour of the roof to brown.
	2.	Format the fill colour of the windows to blue.
	3.	Format the fill colour of the door to orange.
	4.	Format the fill colour of the sun to yellow.
	5.	Format the fill colour of the driveway to red.
	6.	Add three text boxes to appear with the arrows indicating the parts of the drawing, ie stating **Slate Roof**, **Timber Windows** and **Block Paved Drive**.

৯।৪

Rotate And Flip

Objects such as AutoShapes, lines, arrows including text objects can be rotated. Rotation is measured in degrees. This measurement may also be displayed as the ° symbol. There are 360 degrees in a circle and objects can be rotated full circle or in increments such as 90 degrees or 160 degrees etc.

To apply rotation, select the object and click **Format**, **Object**, **AutoShape** or **Text Box** (depending on the type of object being selected) and select the **Size** tab. This method is used where a specific measurement is required.

Alternatively, select the **Rotation** tool on the Drawing toolbar or select **Draw**, **Rotate** or **Flip** from the **Draw** menu on the drawing toolbar.

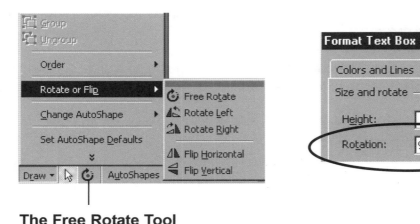

The Free Rotate Tool

To set a specific rotation measurement using the format option from the menu bar, use the up and down arrows or type in the rotation required.

Using the Draw menu to set rotation will rotate an object in increments of 90 degrees.

When clicking the **Free Rotation** tool, rotation handles will appear at each corner of the object.

To rotate, point the mouse pointer at the rotation handle and click and hold the left mouse button.

By clicking and dragging, the object will rotate, either clockwise or anticlockwise, depending on which direction you drag.

T A S K	1. *Apply rotation to the slate roof text box and arrow to 45 degrees.* 2. *Apply rotation to the block paved drive text box and arrow to 30 degrees.*

Grouping Text With Graphical Objects

Grouping

When working with drawn objects on a slide, each object acts as an individual. In some instances, working with the objects one by one is not practical, therefore the 'Group' feature is used.

Grouping objects together has the added benefit of being able to format objects all at once instead of individually.

For example, a flow chart has been created using a mixture of text boxes, shapes and lines. A copy of the flow chart is required on another slide. Instead of individually selecting the objects one by one, the objects can be 'grouped' together. The flow chart becomes one graphical object.

Grouping not only makes cutting and copying objects on a slide simpler, it also eliminates errors in the positioning of the objects.

Objects on a slide include all drawn objects and any images and text. All can be grouped together to make one object.

To group a selection of objects, use one of the following methods:

1. Click **Edit**, **Select All** from the menu bar
    (this is recommended if all objects on the slide
    are to be grouped together).

2. Use the mouse pointer to click and drag around the outside edge of all
    objects to be grouped. On release of the mouse, the objects will be selected.

3. Click on each object in turn (being careful not to drag), whilst holding down
    the **Shift** key on the keyboard. If you add a component by mistake, click on
    the object once more to de-select it.

Once all drawn objects are selected, locate the Drawing toolbar and click **Draw**, **Group**.

You will notice that the objects have now become one object and a new set of selection handles will appear. The objects can now be copied or moved to another slide or application.

To ungroup the object, click **Draw**, **Ungroup** from the Drawing toolbar.

In the following examples, Fig 16 shows all objects selected on the slide. Fig 17 shows the objects once grouped using **Draw**, **Group** from the Menu bar.

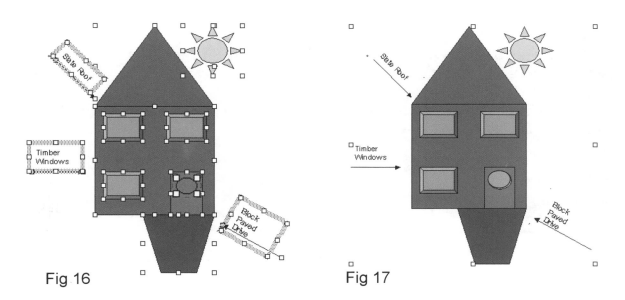

Fig 16   Fig 17

Reposition And Resize Grouped Objects

Grouped objects can be resized and repositioned as with any other inserted object or drawn object. However, you must ensure the objects that have been grouped are formatted correctly.

Once grouped the object will appear with one set of selection handles around it. As with previous sections covering this, the selection handles can be used to resize as necessary.

To resize the grouped object to a specific measurement, select the grouped object and select **Format**, **Object** from the menu bar.

Click on the **Size** tab to insert the measurements as required.

If the grouped object contains text within drawn objects that has been automatically wrapped, the grouped object may not size to your requirements.

To correct this, remove the checks from the options **Word Wrap Text in AutoShape** and **Resize AutoShape to fit Text** appearing in the **Text Box** tab of the dialogue box.

T A S K	1.	*Select all objects in the **House** presentation (except for the title).*
	2.	*Group the objects.*
	3.	*Print slide 1.*
	4.	*Save the changes.*
	5.	*Close the presentation.*

T A S K	1.	Open the existing presentation called **Signs**.
	2.	Group the objects to make one.
	3.	Remove the **Word Wrap** and **Automatically Fit Text** options from the grouped object.
	4.	Resize the grouped object so that the overall object is large enough to display the text in each arrowhead.
	5.	Print slide 1 in pure black and white.
	6.	Save the changes to the presentation. Close the presentation.

Layering

When adding objects to a slide, they are automatically 'layered', for example:

Notice that the star is behind the smiley face and this is behind the arrow; they are in **layers**.

To change the order of an object appearing on a slide, firstly select the object and then use the **Drawing** toolbar.

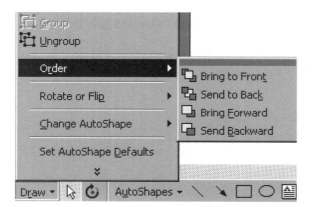

To send the arrow to the back of the smiley face but in front of the star, select it and click on **Draw**, **Order**, **Send Backward**.

The Arrow will now appear like this:

Bring to Front brings the selected object to the front (top) of the layered objects.
Send to Back sends the selected object to the back (bottom) of the layered objects.
Bring Forward brings the selected object one layer forwards.
Send Backward sends the selected object one layer backwards.

T A S K

1. Open a new blank presentation using a blank AutoLayout.

2. Draw several objects on the slide and practise layering each.

3. Close without saving.

31/8

C O N S O L I D A T I O N   E X E R C I S E

1. Open the presentation **United Kingdom**.

2. Add a new slide to make slide 4 and select the title only AutoLayout.

3. Add the title **Major Physical Features**.

4. Draw a triangle on the left side of the slide below the title placeholder.

5. Copy the triangle and position the copy to the right of the original. Resize to appear slightly smaller.

6. Add a text box below the large triangle and insert the text:

   Highest Point Ben Nevis 1344m

7. Format the text to Arial, size 18 pt.

8. Add a second text box to the right of the previous and insert the text:

   Lowest Point Holme Fen - 3m

9. Format the font to match the existing text box.

10. Ensure all slides have the same background colour.

11. Print the presentation as handouts, vertically, 4 per page.

12. Save the changes.

13. Close the presentation.

31/8 .

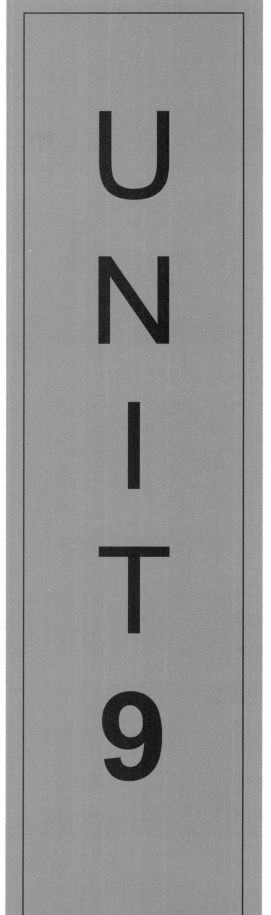

On completion of this unit you will have learnt about and practised the following:

- **Importing Data From Other Applications**

- **Tabs**

- **Indents**

- **Spell Checking**

  - Language
  - Document Checking

 ©Tektra TEKPG1RP1102

Importing Data From Other Applications

The definition of 'import' is to place a file or data which has been created in one application in to another application. The file must be in a format the new application can read, or the new application must have the relevant 'converters' or 'filters' installed.

Converters and filters can be selected when installing Microsoft Office 2000, if the correct options are chosen. If these functions are not present, certain applications may not read particular files.

Using import will enable you to import a whole document created in another application, such as Microsoft Word 2000. An alternative method is to use the copy and paste functions to copy selected text only.

For example: you have created a word processed document using Microsoft Word 2000. You now wish to turn this document into a PowerPoint presentation. However, you do not wish to type in the text again. It is possible to 'import' the document into PowerPoint provided all the necessary converters and filters are present.

To **Import** an existing Word document:

- Open PowerPoint and select **Blank Presentation**.

- Select **File**, **Open** from the menu bar, the **Open** dialogue box will appear.

- Change the **Files of Type** to read **All Files** and other file types will be listed.

- Select the Word Document and click **Open**.

PowerPoint will read the document* and put the information into an order it thinks is appropriate. The presentation will appear in Outline View. Some editing and formatting may be required as the order may not suit your requirements.

*providing all converters and filters are installed and present.

An alternative method is to **Import selected text** only from the Word document.

- Open the word processing software.

- Open the Word document containing the text required.

- Open a new blank presentation in PowerPoint or have open an existing presentation to import the text into.

- **Highlight** or **select** the text to import and click on the **Copy** button.

- Navigate back to PowerPoint and **select** the **slide** to import the text onto.

- Click on the **Paste** button and the text will appear.

The selected text has been imported into the presentation.

The above method can be used between any of the Microsoft Office 2000 applications, ie Microsoft Excel and Access 2000. The applications are designed to be 'integrated' together.

TASK

1. *Open a new blank presentation using a blank AutoLayout.*

2. *Import the Word Document called **PowerPoint 2000**.*

3. *Format the slide background to a light shade of green.*

4. *Insert a new slide to make slide 2.*

5. *Move the text **Getting Help from the Help Menu** from slide 1 to slide 2.*

6. *Position the text towards the top of the slide.*

7. *Open the word processing document called **PowerPoint 2000** in the word processing application (ie Microsoft Word) and copy all text appearing below the section headed '**Getting Help....**' into slide 2 below the title.*

8. *Format both title fonts to Arial, size 40pt in bold.*

9. *Format all sub-title text to Arial, size 20pt.*

10. *Save the presentation as **PP2000**.*

11. *Print both slides and close.*

31/8-

Please note: The Word document contains errors which will be addressed in this unit.

Tabs

Tabs are positions along the ruler and are used when data needs to be displayed in list or column form. Tabs help align data on each line. The **Tab** key is located on the keyboard (*fourth key up on the left side of the keyboard, with arrows pointing left and right*) and is used to get you to the tab stop positions.

When using tabs in presentations, it is important to display the ruler, as tab stop positions will display on the ruler.

There are four different types of tab stops.

You can set your own tab stop positions or you can accept the 'default' tab stop positions.

Tab types

To align	Click
Left edge of text with tab	L
Center of text with tab	⊥
Right edge of text with tab	⌐
Decimal points in text with tab	⊥

Default tabs

A 'default' with regard to computer terms is a preset preference that is used by an application, a 'fallback' position. For example, when first opening Microsoft PowerPoint 2000, the application is set to use a specific font and font size. These are 'defaults' and are used until changed.

This works in the same way with tabs. PowerPoint contains certain tab stop positions to use until a new tab stop position is set.

Tab stop positions can be determined by clicking within a text box or placeholder and pressing the tab key on the keyboard. Once added tabs are set, default tabs are cancelled out.

An example of using tabs:

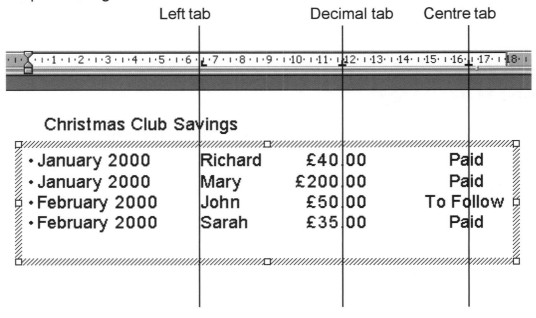

Notice that the first column of data did not require a tab to be set as this information was typed against the bullet point.

•   The first tab used was a left tab.

•   The second tab used was a decimal tab. (Used for any data typed which contains a decimal point.)

•   The third tab used was a centre tab. All data is lined centrally in this column.

Setting custom tab stop positions

1. Ensure you are clicked inside the text box where data is to be tabbed. (The ruler bar will appear differently for every object on the slide.)

2. Locate the '**Tab**' button to the left of the horizontal ruler and above the vertical ruler.

3. By clicking on this button, the tab types will change to either left, right, centre or decimal. It is important to select the correct type of tab.

4. Once the tab has been selected, locate the appropriate position on the horizontal ruler bar where the tab is to be set.

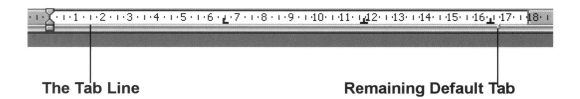

The Tab Line   **Remaining Default Tab**

5. By clicking with the left mouse button on the rulers tab line, the tab will show. Any tabs you have set will cancel out the default tabs up to that point. After that, default tabs will appear.

Removing or clearing tabs

Tabs can be removed by clicking and holding the tab with the left mouse button and dragging off or sliding off the ruler bar.

Alternatively, use the **Undo** button on the toolbar.

Indents

Indentation can be set for individual or multiple paragraphs and lines of text. It is the distance between the left edge of the text from the margin of a text box or placeholder.

The examples below show how indentation can be applied. To apply indentation, ensure the ruler is visible by selecting **View**, **Ruler** from the menu bar. Click into a piece of text in a box or placeholder to view the indentation markers on the ruler. To move the markers, click on them with the left mouse button and 'drag' to the required position.

The indent markers will indicate if any indentation has been applied to text.

The upper marker is called the **First Line** indent.

This is a piece of text which has a First line indent applied at a position of 1cm on the Ruler.

The lower marker refers to other lines in a paragraph of text. This is known as a **Hanging** indent.

This is a piece of text which has an indent applied at a position of 1cm on the Ruler to all lines except for the first line.

To apply an indent and retain all lines in the paragraph, move both markers by dragging the rectangular part of the lower marker.

This is a piece of text which has an indent applied at a position of 1cm on the Ruler to all lines.

T A S K

1. Open the presentation called **Project V1**.

2. Add a new slide to make slide 8 and select a bulleted list AutoLayout.

3. Add the title **Workshop Schedule** and format the font to Tahoma, size 40pt.

4. Set appropriate tab stop positions for the text below.

5. Remove the bullet point and add the text below in tabbed format. Change the font to Tahoma size 24pt.

February	5th	19th	24th	14.00 hrs
March	12th	18th	21st	15.00 hrs
April	9th	11th	18th	09.00 hrs
May	8th	10th	20th	13.00 hrs

6. Apply a 1cm indent to all lines in the sub-title text on slides 5 and 6.

7. Print slides 5, 6 and 8 only in black and white.

8. Save the changes to the presentation.

1/9

 ©Tektra TEKPG1RP1102

Spell Checking

All presentations should be checked for spelling errors. This is sometimes known as proofing. PowerPoint 2000 has a facility to do just this and checks each word in your document against a standard dictionary. If a word is unknown to the dictionary, it will be 'flagged' by the appearance of a red wavy line underneath the word (if this feature is activated).

Either check the whole presentation or a selection which has been highlighted. If checking the whole presentation, ensure you are viewing Slide 1 of the presentation.

To activate the spell checker, either use the button on the toolbar:

or select **Tools**, **Spelling** from the menu bar.

The **Spelling** Dialogue Box

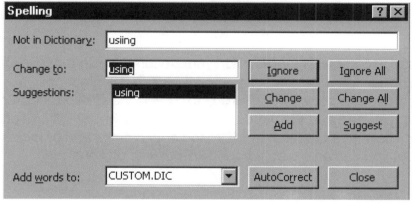

The unrecognised word will appear together with a recommendation of what to change the spelling to. The spell checker will also offer other spelling suggestions.

Fig 18

Ignore	Skips the highlighted word without making changes
Ignore All	Skips over all occurrences of the word
Change	Replaces the original word with the suggestion
Change All	Replaces all occurrences of the word with the suggestion
Add	Adds the typed word to the dictionary
Suggest	Displays other suggestions from the dictionary

The spell checker may not recognise names of people or places. These would need to be manually checked and then added to the dictionary if you use them regularly.

To proceed to check the presentation, one of the above buttons must be selected for the checker to move onto the next word.

If there are spelling errors in your presentations the **Spelling** dialogue box will be displayed (see previous page). However, if the presentation contains no spelling errors, the following message will be displayed:

Fig 19

Once the spell checker reaches the end of the document, it will also display the message as in Fig 19. Click **OK** to this message to close the spell checker.

Language

When the spell checker is used, it compares the words in your document with those in its main dictionary. The main dictionary contains most common words, but it might not include proper names, technical terms, acronyms, and so on. To prevent the spelling checker from questioning such words, you can add the words to a custom dictionary. Microsoft PowerPoint 2000 shares its dictionary with the other Microsoft applications and provides a built-in custom dictionary, but you can also create your own 'custom' dictionaries.

The custom dictionary will be assigned a language; this will be dependant on which options were selected at the time of installation of the application. There are many languages available in the Microsoft applications.

To view the language being used, select **Tools**, **Language** from the menu bar to activate the **Language** dialogue box.

Select the language required and the spell checker and other tools will automatically check documents using this language.

<u>Document Checking</u>

Once you have completed a document it is important to perform certain checks to ensure that it is free from errors. Using a spell checker can quickly eliminate any spelling errors electronically, but it will not pick up certain styles of typing, such as typing 'you' instead of 'your'. The spell checker recognises both of these words as correct, therefore your document will need to be proofread manually to check the meaning of words in sentences. Check documents for accuracy of information and correctness where possible.

Final checks should include the following:

Spell checking (against the correct language)
Grammar checking
Correctness of information and meanings
Printed outcome (Print Preview for accuracy and layout)
Factually correct information

T A S K

1. *Check the spelling in the **Project V1** presentation (names of people and places can be ignored).*

2. *Check the spelling in the **PP2000** presentation and correct any errors.*

3. *Save the changes to both presentations.*

4. *Close both presentations.*

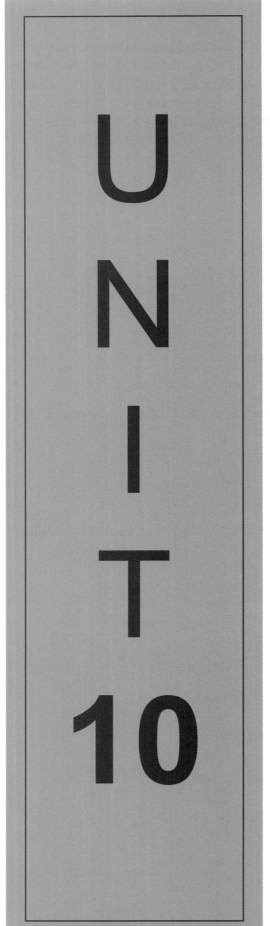

On completion of this unit you will have learnt about and practised the following:

- **Viewing A Presentation As A Slide Show**

  - Slide Show Control Shortcuts

 ©Tektra TEKPG1RP1102

Viewing A Presentation As A Slide Show

Throughout the book, various tasks have been instructing you to click on the **Slide Show** button to view as a show. However, this unit will look into the options available whilst viewing the show.

Once you have activated a show you must navigate between slides to view the show. So far, you have learned that by clicking the left mouse button or using the spacebar on the keyboard, you can advance between slides.

Other options include:

Clicking the right mouse button to view the **Slide Show shortcut menu** (or pop-up menu) and clicking the left mouse button to select commands.

Clicking the **navigation button** (which will display when the mouse is moved) in the bottom left corner of the slide.

Another method is to use the available **keyboard shortcuts** (see back of book for details).

The navigation button

When clicked with the left mouse button, the **Navigation** button will display options. Using the left or right mouse button, click on the option that you require.

Next and Previous

Navigate to the next and previous slides with these buttons.

The Go sub-menu

Available options are **Slide Navigator** and **By Title**. Both of these options enable you to pick out the slide to navigate to, either by number or by name.

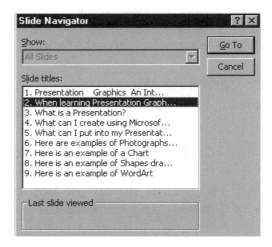

Meeting Minder

Meeting minder enables you to add minutes of the meeting and action points as you navigate through the presentation show. This feature also has a facility to link to a scheduler (diary) for keeping track of appointments. If required, the minutes and action points can be exported to Microsoft Word from here. If adding action points, a new slide is created at the end of the show, summarising the action points required. This is a useful tool as a copy of the action points can be taken away at the end of a meeting.

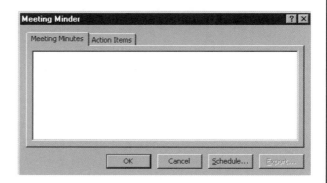

Speaker Notes

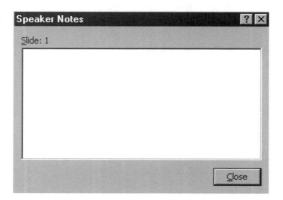

Speaker notes can be added slide by slide as the presentation is running. Right click and select **Speaker Notes** from the menu.

However, you may wish to add speaker notes before the presentation is shown to an audience. You can create annotations and information for the speaker to refer to whilst the show is running.

Pointer Options

Select the type of mouse pointer to use with the presentation. By default, the arrow will appear automatically. If you would like to use the annotation pen as the mouse pointer in the presentation, select the pen option. This will enable you to write on the presentation, for example you can circle key points as you are talking about them.

Pointer options will enable you to choose to hide the pointer. Pen colours can be selected from a range of standard colours and reset if required.

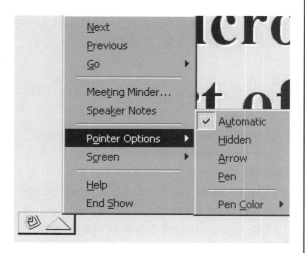

Fig 20

Fig 20 is an example of using the pen as the mouse pointer.

By using the mouse, key sections of a presentation can be highlighted.

To erase any pen annotations, select **Screen**, **Erase Pen** from the navigation button.

Screen

The screen option will set the screen to black if required, erase any pen annotations and pause the presentation.

T A S K	1.	*Open the **Project V1** presentation.*
	2.	*View the presentation as a slide show.*
	3.	*Using the mouse as a control method, navigate through the slide show you have created.*
	4.	*Print the whole presentation in black and white, save the changes and close the presentation.*

Slide Show Control Shortcuts

You can use the following shortcuts while running your Slide Show
in full-screen mode.

To	Press
Advance to the next slide	**N**, **Enter**, or the **Spacebar** (or click the mouse)
Return to the previous slide	**P** or **Backspace**
Go to slide <number>	<number>+**Enter**
Display a black screen, or return to the slide show from a black screen	**B**
Display a white screen, or return to the slide show from a white screen	**W**
Stop or restart an automatic slide show	**S**
End a slide show	**Esc**
Erase on-screen annotations	**E**
Go to next hidden slide	**H**
Set new timings while rehearsing	**T**
Use original timings while rehearsing	**O**
Use mouse-click to advance while rehearsing	**M**
Return to the first slide	Both mouse buttons for 2 seconds
Change the pointer to a pen	**Ctrl+P**
Change the pen to a pointer	**Ctrl+A**
Hide the pointer and button temporarily	**Ctrl+H**
Hide the pointer and button always	**Ctrl+L**
Display the shortcut menu	**Shift+F10** (or right-click)

C O N S O L I D A T I O N   E X E R C I S E

1.   Read through the scenario below. Then follow further instructions on the next page.

Scenario:

You are working for Outsource Ltd, a company who carry out motivation workshops for businesses. Your Supervisor has instructed you to put together an introductory presentation to be given at the start of the workshops. You have been advised to use Clip Art where appropriate and to spell check the presentation on completion (ignoring any people or place names). Your Supervisor has suggested content for the slides. Construct the presentation and consider slide layouts required. It is recommended to use a template format for the presentation to ensure consistency.

Slide 1   Outsource Limited
                       A presentation by [insert your name here]

Slide 2   An Introduction
                       Outsource Ltd was formed in 1988.

                       We offer Motivation Workshops to businesses
                       who believe their Staff Morale would benefit.

Slide 3   Instructors
                       Outsource Ltd have three instructors:

                       Stephen Wyatt
                       Jeremy Jones
                       Terry Parker

                       All of whom have been in the business for 20 years.

Slide 4   Workshops
                       Motivation Workshops are structured to include:

                       Brain storming sessions
                       Role play
                       Discussion forums
                       Feedback
                       Summary

Slide 5   Conclusion
                       On completion of the Motivation Workshop we aim to
                       enhance your working life and make the workplace a
                       fun motivated environment to work in!

CONSOLIDATION EXERCISE

Instructions continued:

2. *Ensure that you have read the previous page thoroughly.*

3. *Open the presentation graphics application.*

3. *Create a new presentation using a suitable design template.*

4. *Using the information from the scenario, produce a suitable presentation. The following additional notes should be adhered to:*

   Use at least two suitable Clip Art images.
   Use bullet points where necessary.
   Use at least two types of text formatting.

5. *Check the spelling for the whole presentation (names of people and places can be ignored).*

6. *Save the presentation as **Outsource MW**.*

7. *Print the presentation as handouts, 6 per page, horizontally and in black and white.*

8. *View the presentation as a slide show, save and close.*

CONSOLIDATION EXERCISE

1.   Read through the scenario below.   Then follow further instructions on page 107.

Scenario:

As an employee of Outsource Ltd you have been instructed to compile a presentation from a strict brief.

The presentation involves giving local talks on various subjects to local residents. The first talk is on the subject of photography.   You have been provided with sample content (see below) for the slides and a collection of photographic images to use in the presentation. It is important that the presentation be checked thoroughly before being given to ensure accuracy.   Construct the presentation, taking into consideration the content required. Use a template format from those available.

Slide 1   Outsource Limited
               A Local Initiative Presentation by [your name here]

Slide 2   Introduction
               Local Initiative Presentations – bringing local communities together.

Slide 3   Photography

               We will cover:

               Photography Insight
               Types of Camera
               Lenses
               Accessories
               Practical session of example photographs

Slide 4   Photography Insight

               One item of equipment held in most households is a camera, whether this is for occasional photography, a serious hobby or professional use.

               It is hard to imagine any person who has not ever appeared in a photograph. Photographs provide us with a way of capturing moments in time forever.

               Cameras are available in many ranges, from the most complex to the most sophisticated.

               This presentation is designed to offer information on the various options available when involved in photography.

C O N S O L I D A T I O N   E X E R C I S E

Slide 5   Types of Camera

What type of camera is best for me?

The 35mm Camera; The Single Reflex Camera (SLR);
The Rangefinder Camera; The SLR Medium Format Camera;
The 5 x 4 Camera; The Instant or Polaroid Camera; The Video
Still Camera

Slide 6   Lenses

Having a choice of camera types is enough, however, there is also a
wide range of lenses available for every eventuality.

Standard Lens (used on most 35mm SLR Cameras)
Focal length 50m (approx)
Angle of view equal to that of the human eye (approx)

Interchangeable Lenses
Wide angle lenses – wider angle of view
Telephoto lenses – brings distant objects closer
Zoom lenses – better quality of composition
Fisheye lenses – used to add a dramatic effect
Macro lenses – used for extreme close ups

Slide 7   Accessories

So you have purchased a camera, a couple of lenses, and now there
is a range of accessories to buy!

UV Filters	Reduces the amount of ultra-violet light passing through the camera.
The Lens Hood	Prevents stray light from entering the camera.
A Tripod	Keeps the camera steady.
A Monopod	Used to keep the camera steady, however has only one leg for ease of transportation.
A Carry Case	Provides protection for expensive equipment.

Slide 8   Practical Session

   ©Tektra TEKPG1RP1102

CONSOLIDATION EXERCISE

Instructions:

1.   *Read the scenario carefully and consider the layout required.*

2.   *Open the presentation graphics application.*

3.   *Create a new presentation using a design template and select an appropriate slide layout for slide 1.*

4.   *Add the text for slide 1 using the font Arial and format to a suitable size. Use this font throughout the remainder of the presentation. Add your own name where indicated.*

5.   *Create slide 2. Align the sub-title text centred horizontally below the slide heading. Add the image from disk called **People**, resize and position below the sub-title text and centre horizontally.*

6.   *Create slide 3. Apply bullet points to the items the presentation will cover. Resize the font in the bulleted list if necessary to suit the slide layout. The bulleted list should be left aligned. Apply bold and italics to the heading of the bulleted list 'We will cover:'*

7.   *Create slide 4. Apply a hanging indent at 2cm to all paragraphs. Ensure all text fits on the slide to suit the layout and adjust the font size if necessary.*

8.   *Create slide 5. Insert a Clip Art image from those available of a camera. Position to the right of the slide title and resize if necessary. Apply bullet points to the list of cameras available. Apply bold to the heading of the bulleted list.*

9.   *Create slide 6. Apply bullet points to the two main items in the list ie **Standard Lens** and **Interchangeable Lenses**. Format the bulleted list heading to Italics.*

10. *Create slide 7. Use a suitable tab stop position to type the list. Format the accessory headings to bold and a different colour, which should stand out from the slide background.*

11. *Create slide 8. Insert the 4 images from disk: **Night**; **Dice**; **Shadow** and **Landscape**. Place in a suitable position on the slide, resizing if necessary. Add a rounded rectangle AutoShape below the first image. Format the fill colour to a light shade of blue. Copy the AutoShape three times and place one below each image. Use a suitable method to add text to the rectangles to indicate the name of each image. Ensure that the font appears in a text colour which stands out.*

12. *Check the whole presentation thoroughly, correcting any spelling errors (names of people or places can be ignored).*

Continued over the page...

C
O
N
S
O
L
I
D
A
T
I
O
N

E
X
E
R
C
I
S
E

13. *Save the presentation with the name **Photography**.*

14. *Print slide 1 only in black and white.*

15. *Print slides 2–8 as handouts (9 per page), horizontally in black and white.*

16. *View the presentation as a slide show, save any changes and close.*

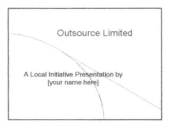

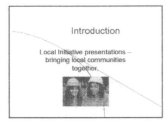

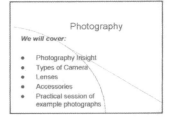

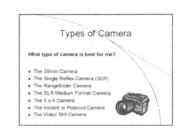

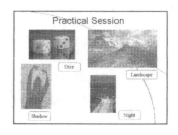

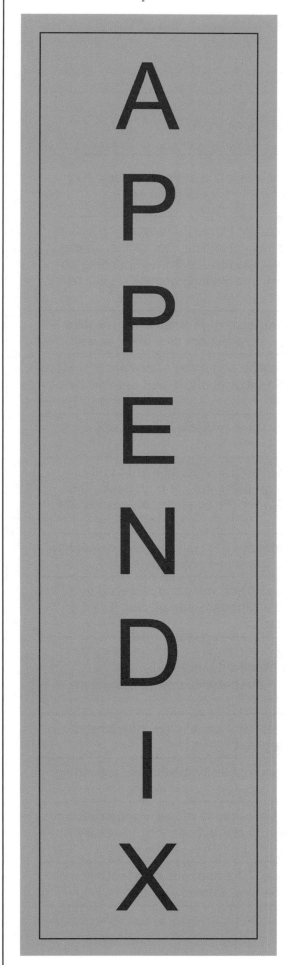

- **Glossary Of Terms**

GLOSSARY

Animation	The movement of any object on a slide.
Application	Software program which carries out a specific activity, such as word processing, spreadsheets or databases.
AutoContent Wizard	A selection option when starting PowerPoint, enabling you to create a presentation already containing information. There are many different categories to choose from depending on the type of presentation you are creating and the audience it will be shown to.
AutoLayout	Layout designs of slides depending on whether you require text only, text and graphics, bulleted lists or a blank screen.
Bullet point	A bullet point is a marker at the beginning of an item in a list used to define them. Different symbols can be used as bullet points.
Clip Art	A library of pictures and images available for use with Microsoft applications.
Clipboard	An area of the computer's memory used as a temporary storage area when text or graphics are cut or copied. The clipboard is not seen and when the computer is switched off, its contents are lost.
Colour scheme	A palette of colours available for use with your presentation to change background, text, shape and line colours.
Copy	When making a copy of an object, you are duplicating it, temporarily placing it on the clipboard and placing it elsewhere in your presentation.
Cut	When cutting an object, you are removing it from its current location, placing it on the clipboard temporarily, and positioning it elsewhere in your presentation, ie moving the object.
Default setting	A value, action or setting that is automatically used when no alternative instructions are given.
Demote	Making a point in a list stand out less than the line preceding it.
Effect	Adding an effect to an object or piece of text, eg animation or movement or to make the object a different colour, texture or pattern.
Font	Also referred to as typeface. The appearance of your printed characters ie Arial or Times New Roman.

Gradient fill	Using a gradient colour means to start out at one part of the slide as one colour but eventually becoming two.
Graph	A chart window, including the legend (key), the chart itself, the title of the chart etc.
Graphics	Graphics are objects placed into the presentation and can be in different formats, depending on how they were created. Graphics can be pictures, charts, photographs etc.
Group	A set of objects grouped together to make one, easier for copying and cutting.
Handles	Handles, sometimes referred to as 'selection handles', are the small white squares that appear around an object when selected. They are used for resizing objects to make them larger or smaller.
Internet	A network of computers all over the world linked to each other to communicate.
Intranet	An in-house internet, with restricted access, ie for company employees only
Object	Items which appear on a slide. These can include text, charts, pictures and photographs.
Orientation	A setting which tells the printer which way to print on paper. If the wide edge is at the top, this is landscape, if the narrow edge is at the top, this is portrait.
Paste	When clicking on paste, whatever has been placed on the clipboard last will appear on the screen.
Placeholder	A box appearing on a slide in which graphics text or other objects can be placed.
Promote	Making a point in a list stand out more than the line preceding it.
Slide background	The area that appears behind all objects on a slide. This area can be customized to have a different colour, texture, pattern, photograph or gradient.
Tab	Horizontal points along the ruler bar used for aligning text.
Template	A set of presentation designs which are part of the PowerPoint program.
Text box	A placeholder for text on a slide. Text boxes can be drawn at any time and text inserted into them.
Transition	A system of moving from one slide to another. This may include a special effect such as vertical or horizontal blinds.
Wizard	A set of step by step screens within a program which make it easier to perform an action. The wizard will create presentations for you.

This Page is

intentionally

Left Blank